ROOKIE

Surviving Your First Year of College Softball

By

FRED DOHRMANN

With

DAN BLANK

For June…everything we talked about over the years, is now in writing. Thanks for being a great listener.

If you would like to place a bulk order of twenty or more copies of ROOKIE at a discounted price, just email me at softballcoachfred@gmail.com.

Contents

FOREWORD

I'd like to congratulate you on making a very good investment. Because that's what ROOKIE should be to you —an investment.

Think about what you've given to softball to reach this moment: The countless hours over many years. The running, the throwing, the swinging. The times you bravely squared up to a bouncing ball that seemed to be leaving a vapor trail in its wake. The sore arms and ice packs and raspberries. The thousands of miles. All those trips to practices, games, camps, college visits and individual lessons. The bats and gloves and cleats. The fast food. The late nights of laundry. The stress of the recruiting process. The money. You've given a lot to this game.

For parents and players, the investment in time and dollars can run deep. We strive for the development of the high school athlete's skill set —to help them reach varsity, and from there, the college level of the game. Being prepared, making the most of that investment, and squeezing every last drop of possibility into a student-athlete's efforts is at the root of this guide by Coach Dohrmann.

I've been privileged to really know Coach Dohrmann for over a decade —but I knew *of* him professionally for many years prior, in my role as coach, recruiting director, and involvement with fastpitch softball on a national level. Fred is a Philly guy, a straight shooter, who revels in the plain, simple, direct and positive approach to life that values hard work. His love affair with sports in general, and Widener Athletics in particular, is no surprise. Fred has been an iconic figure on campus for over 42 years! Hundreds of young women have been positively impacted by this man's kind and caring devotion to this school and its students.

He would be the last one to tell you this, but Coach Dohrmann's 697 wins rank 22nd all-time in NCAA Division III history, with sixteen 20-win seasons, and countless all-conference players and NFCA all-academic athletes. If you haven't figured it out yet, yeah, this guy knows his stuff!

Think of this book as your BEST investment. It will complete your softball portfolio. Yet, every investor must be an active participant to maximize returns. The Do's and Don'ts are clearly laid out in the coming pages. Eat this up, digest it, and put it into action, and I promise you that your college softball experience will surpass any expected investment returns!

Frank Ehrenfeld,
Pennsbury Gems - Director of Recruiting,
NFCA Board of Directors, 2022-2024

PREFACE

When word got out that my university had just hired a new soccer coach who also happened to be a best-selling author, I was naturally curious. I was a soccer guy way back when, so I decided to do a quick Google on Coach Dan Blank. Eventually I landed on his catalog of books and, not surprisingly, most of his titles were soccer-specific and wouldn't do me much good in my role as Head Softball Coach at Widener University. But there were a few titles that had the potential for a crossover audience, and one of those books was called *Rookie —Surviving Your Freshman Year of College Soccer*. Great title. I had to check it out.

I was delighted that so many of the lessons in Rookie seemed universal to college athletes and could be applied well beyond soccer. And although I was reading Dan's book, it was my voice I heard saying those words. As I read that book I thought, 'There needs to be a version of this book for softball players. They need as much help as anyone!'

So, Dan and I collaborated to create the book you are now reading, and it's something we're both proud of. Incidentally, if you want to read any of Dan's other books, I highly recommend starting with *Everything Your Coach Never Told You Because You're a Girl*. It's an eye-opener!

One note of housekeeping before we begin… I understand that gender identification is an important topic. I'm completely on board with the cultural shift to greater inclusivity. And if we ever meet in person, I'll be happy to honor whatever pronouns you prefer. However, in the interest of creating the most readable product for the largest likely audience, we have stuck with the traditional feminine pronouns of she/her/hers when referring to softball players. When referring to coaches, we've done our best to alternate chapters between male and female coaches, and again, stuck with the traditional pronouns.

I hope you understand our choices and enjoy this book.

~ Fred Dohrmann

INTRODUCTION

Abraham Lincoln once said, "Give me six hours to chop down a tree and I'll spend the first four sharpening the axe." Honest Abe knew that there's no substitute for preparation.

You are about to embark on one of the most incredible and memorable adventures your life will ever offer. You're about to become a college softball player. Congratulations! It truly is a once-in-a-lifetime opportunity and believe me, it will go by much faster than you could ever imagine. Four or five years from now, in the final inning of your final game, an umpire will call someone out and - *just like that!* - your softball career will be finished. The game you love most will have vanished while the sound of the umpire's voice is still hanging in the air. You'll shout up to the heavens for just one more game, but it'll all be gone. And as you bargain with the gods for one more chance to wear that uniform and represent your college or university, you'll look back upon your four years and reflect upon all the things you wish you had done differently. You'll end up wishing that you could've known then what you do know now. You'll retreat to be alone with your sadness, and there in your despair, you will remember that quote from Abe Lincoln. And you'll wish that you had armed yourself with a sharper axe.

At least that's how it used to be. You on the other hand... well, you're different! You've chosen to prepare yourself. You've chosen to arm yourself with knowledge - *with some inside info* - and I commend you for it.

By reading this book, you've chosen to give yourself a head start and a

1

competitive edge. Considering the world you are about to enter is predicated upon competition, any type of head start is a very valuable asset.

I've coached college softball for forty-one years. Among the many things I've learned is this: First-year players struggle. Why? Because they're first-years! Because they are inexperienced. Because they are dropped into a brand new world without the benefit of hindsight and the only way for them to learn is through trial and error, with plenty of error. I've spent four decades observing rookies making the same mistakes over and over again. It's time to put an end to that!

Yes, you're a rookie, but you don't have to be a bewildered one. You can give yourself a fighting chance to sidestep the landmines that have exploded beneath so many of your predecessors. Let this book be your GPS as you navigate your first year of college softball, and you'll be thankful you did.

Here's the deal… It doesn't matter if you're going to a small school or a big one; it doesn't matter what division of college softball you'll be playing; I'm going to give you a lot of excellent advice. You can choose to take it or leave it; that's entirely your call. But if you put your trust in me, I guarantee that your rookie season will go a whole lot smoother and that your chances of success will dramatically improve.

You're about to embark on the best four years of your life. Let's try to make them even better! C'mon Rookie, it's time to sharpen your axe.

SECTION 1

BEFORE YOU GO

1

LEGACY

When you're planning your Spring Break vacation, what's the first and most important decision you have to make? Before you buy your plane ticket or gas up your car or pack your suitcase, you obviously need to pick your destination. Do you need to bring a swimsuit and sun block, or a wool hat and boots? Your destination has a major impact on all of the other choices you're going to make.

You have four seasons of college softball. That's not a lot. When your career is finished, your coaches and teammates will talk about the kind of player you were; about the type of teammate and leader you were; about the type of student and citizen you were. The words they choose to describe you will be your legacy. Ultimately, on this trip that is college softball, your legacy is your destination.

Before you start packing your suitcases, do yourself a tremendous favor and define your legacy. Figure out what your college career is going to look like. Find yourself an hour of quiet and solitude, and pretend that you are a college senior and your softball career has just ended. Looking back, what do you see? Over these past four years, who were you?

What type of player were you? What type of teammate were you? What were the principles that you refused to bend? Were you a leader? Maybe a captain? What were the characteristics that defined you in the eyes of your coaches and teammates? Ask yourself, *"What will they say about me when it's all over?"*

Write it down. Read it. Write it down again. Write down your destination and keep it close to you. Refer to it often. Use it to guide your decisions on and off the field. Decide who you will be and how you'll be remembered and then live the life that you've envisioned.

Your legacy doesn't start during your senior season. Your legacy begins the moment you step foot onto that campus. And it's too important to leave to chance. Define the player and person you are going to be *before* you get to college. Pick your destination before you get in the car and go. It just makes better sense, right?

Leave a legacy that is worthy of you. You'll never regret it. I promise.

2
GOALS

As you define and design your legacy, it's only natural that you will set some goals for yourself. Fantastic! You should have athletic goals and academic goals and goals for whatever else inspires you. Speaking from a strictly softball standpoint, let me give you a few worthwhile goals for your freshman year. You can tweak them however you like and you are welcome to add others, but these will give you a running start.

- Make the roster and the travel squad for the first away trip.
  Don't get left behind, get on the roster. A little bit later you'll read about the tiers of a college softball team, but for now let's just say that if you want to get in the game, you first have to *go* to the game. Being in the travel squad gets you in the hunt.

- Get on the field.
  Playing college softball is a lot more fun than watching college softball. Do what you need to do to get on the field, even as a reserve. It may mean changing the way you play. It may mean changing your position. Stay flexible and do what you need to do to get in the game.

- Be a great teammate.
  Be the type of teammate that you would like to have. Help your

teammates before they ask. Do more than your fair share of the things that aren't as much fun.

- Earn the respect of your coaches.
  These are the folks who decide if and how much you'll play. Show them that you are someone who deserves to be taken seriously.

- Own your academics.
  Plan to get to your first college class (locate the classroom beforehand so you are on time) and have 100% attendance. Have all your homework completed and turned in on time. Aim for a 4.0 GPA.

If you can reach these goals, then there's a pretty good chance that you'll consider your rookie season a success. If you win yourself a starting position right out of the gate, that's even better!

3

THE BUBBLE

When I was seventeen, I couldn't wait to get out of my house and on to college! I was obsessed with the idea of sweet freedom –the chance to set my own rules and be my own person and drink from the cup of independence! College was going to totally rock! And believe me, it totally did.

If you have a similar outlook on college, let me tell you a little secret that I wish someone had told me: College is a lot smaller than you think, especially if you're an athlete.

College is a bubble. It's a sort of parallel universe that you get to inhabit for four or five years with hundreds or thousands of others, and regardless of how many others share your bubble, it's a bubble nonetheless, and that means all the inhabitants are in some way connected. And in that bubble, word travels, and it travels fast. Very few secrets survive inside the bubble. Remember that.

You are an athlete. That makes you high-profile regardless of the sport you play and regardless of the success of your team. You get to enjoy a certain double-standard. You'll get some free clothing and some nice meals and the chance to travel. You might even get an athletic scholarship. But most and best of all, you'll get to represent your university in the throes of competition. People will watch you and cheer for you. You'll be a celebrity inside that bubble. Plenty of people will know your name, and many people who don't know your name will simply refer to you as someone who is *on the softball team. Softball player* will become your identity. Some people will love you for it and others will dislike you because of it, but *everyone* will be talking about you if you give them the chance. This is the price of your celebrity.

Incidentally, don't kid yourself that the bubble only applies to schools of a certain size. I've coached at a school of 2700 and was a student-athlete at a university of 25,000, and I assure you, even big schools are small.

You have only one reputation and it is one of the very few things that is 100% yours. Take care of it. Protect it. Guard it with pride and honor. As an athlete you live at the top. The view from up there is much nicer, but the fall hurts twice as much.

And while we are speaking of your reputation, let me remind you that social media shrinks the bubble even further. I and many other college coaches and college athletes will attest that social media is not your friend. From here on out, every status update you post or message you tweet or Tik you Tok represents far more than just you. You are now representing your teammates, coaches and your university. Something that is funny to you might not seem so comical to the athletic director or the university president. And once you put it out there, you can't get it back.

If you're having a bad day and need to vent, there's no law that says you must do so in a public forum. Have the maturity to exercise good judgment. The world doesn't need to know about every one of your perceived injustices, so find another way to blow off your steam.

There are parts of your life that are better kept private. Don't risk social media ruin because a week later you'll realize how stupid and trivial your declaration seems in hindsight. Coaches and administrators aren't very forgiving when it comes to social media, so handle it with caution and care.

We live in a time where everyone has a camera in their pocket. Keep yourself out of compromising situations and your worries will be fewer. Pictures of you dancing at a frat party wearing your team tee-shirt won't do you any favors. When it comes to pictures, perception becomes reality. What actually happened takes a backseat to what appears to be happening. And just to give you a heads-up, if you're photographed holding a red plastic cup, your coach is going to assume that it's filled with alcohol. So will everyone else. That's just the way the world spins. It's an argument that you will never win, so you're better off just avoiding it altogether.

Our alcohol policy was no drinking twenty-four hours before a game. One of our starters went home the night before a double header and had an awesome homemade pasta dinner with her pop's very special, homemade sauce. I won't argue that the dish cried out for a glass of homemade red wine. The player was twenty-one, and personally, I had no problem with her indulging in a small glass of wine, in private, with her family. Unfortunately, instead of keeping it private, she made the very rookie mistake of broadcasting it, posting a photo of that glass of wine in her social media. My assistant coach saw the post about six seconds later and we were left with no choice but to bench the player. It was a textbook case of a self-inflicted, social-media wound. Be mindful of what you post.

There are all types of landmines inside the bubble. Navigate them with care. In the end, you really just have to ask yourself if you want to be taken seriously as an athlete. If you want others to take you seriously, then you have to first take yourself seriously. In short, get past the party. The sooner the better.

4

MAKE
RELATIONSHIPS

Imagine this: It's the opening morning of the fall season and the very first thing you encounter is a weight-room session. You look at the teammate to your left, then the teammate to your right. You realize that you don't know either of their names, yet here you are, on your first day of college softball, competing against them for a chance to represent your university. Your days will be filled with moments just like this, competing against strangers —competing against fellow rookies trying to get noticed, and against returning players who are fighting to hold onto their positions and who view you as a threat.

It wasn't so long ago that the first day of fall preseason was like that for almost every rookie. Teammates were adversaries before they were friends. For plenty of first-years, it still looks like that; but it doesn't have to.

In this book you're going to read a lot about returning players. Don't worry, some of them will become your best friends. But that's somewhere down the road. For now, let me tell you something very important about returners: They are territorial. If a player was a starter last year, she feels entitled to start this year. If she didn't start but the starter graduated, she feels as though she is entitled to that spot because she waited her turn. Your coach won't share those views on entitlement, but that's irrelevant right now, because all that returning player cares about is protecting what's hers like a Mama Bear. You're a threat, and when it comes to softball, she'd just as soon eat you.

One of the best things you can do to help your own cause is to develop a friendship before you start competing against her. If you don't, then on the day you meet, you'll be meeting as adversaries. That's a tough foundation for building a relationship, and it's a tough way to gain acceptance into the team.

When the fall preseason opens, you want to have some allies in the returning classes. You want some of those players to know you and to like you because they'll be your guardian angels and your passport. If they like you, they'll get you inside the club. I cannot possibly overstate how important this can be.

How can you build a relationship before the fall preseason? Well, how about enrolling in summer school? A lot of returning players spend their summers *in town*. You can take a class or two, earn a few quick credits and be left with an abundance of time to learn your surroundings and develop friendships with your future teammates.

Summer camps are another excellent relationship builder. Most college coaches run softball camps and many of the players serve as camp coaches. See if the coach will hire you for a few weeks during the summer. Camp staffs tend to bond very well. There's something about trying to manage a group of 150 small children that leads to the birth of beautiful friendships.

If you can't get yourself physically connected to your teammates, then use phone calls, email and social media to build your relationships. Hopefully you spent the night with a player when you visited campus. Stay in touch with that host and the other players you met. You don't want to be a stranger when you step onto that field, so make the effort to stay connected.

I'm also going to advise you to do some reconnaissance. The internet is a valuable cheat sheet and you should use it to your advantage. Read everything you can about the team. Study the roster. Read the feature stories. Read every post-game article and watch every video. Listen to the interviews. You can learn an awful lot about your future teammates if you just pay attention.

When you show up to the fall preseason or the first meeting of the upcoming year, you want to know everything you can about the returners, starting with their names. *Especially their names!* Have those names committed to memory before you arrive. This will make your life much easier on so many levels.

And since you're doing recon anyway, pay attention to anything the coach says. If you just extract the coach's quotes from a season's worth of articles, you'll have a pretty fantastic idea of what the coach is looking for in his players and how he wants his team to play. This information is completely free. Take advantage of it. It's another great chance to sharpen your axe.

5

PREPARING
FOR
FALL BALL

The fall of your first semester is an audition and no one lives under more scrutiny than the rookies. The returning players want to know what you have to offer and whether or not they should fear you. The coach has seen the returning players for at least a year, so she has a pretty good handle on their abilities. But this is her first chance to closely evaluate you over an extended period of time, so she is going to watch you closely. I want you to take that as wonderful news!

You want to make preseason and fall ball your showcase, and you want to give your coaches and teammates every reason to take you seriously, so let's start out with a few simple pointers.

- Learn to do a proper push-up
  When the coach says, "Ten push-ups," for the love of Pete, don't do them with your knees on the ground. Learn to do proper push-ups, with your fingers pointing forward and your legs, back and neck straight as a beam of lumber. Don't just stay in one position and bob your head up and down like a chicken pecking at feed. Bend your arms to go down and straighten them to go up. You'll

probably never be asked to do more than ten push-ups in a single set, so train yourself to do fifteen proper push-ups.

- Hire a personal trainer for a month
  You can figure out the push-up thing on your own, but when you get to college, you're also going to have to lift weights and do plyometric exercises. I highly recommend that you get some experience with these exercises before you have to do them in front of other people. Have an expert teach you the proper technique for squats and cleans and crunches and pull-ups and lunges and box jumps and all of those other magical exercises that you'll be doing in the near future.

- Lift
  All high-end teams do weight training. Please don't start your lifting in August for a start in early September. Hit the weights as soon as you can, and hopefully no later than mid-June. Be in top form at the first lift.

- Develop your softball IQ
  Watch a lot of softball. The NCAA Division 1 College Softball World Series is broadcast on national TV, and you can find Division 1 replays online. If possible, get someone to film you playing. Identify and eliminate mistakes you're making and your chances of getting on the field will improve. I promise it will help you.

- Become a specialist
  One way to improve your brand and rise above the crowd is to develop a defining quality. As you work to develop all areas of your game, I highly recommend that you also specialize at something. Pick an area that you're already good at and become stupendous at it. Maybe you can steal bases. Maybe you can slap. Maybe you can be an awesome bunter. It doesn't matter what it is, find something that you can be the best at and you will become more marketable to your coach.

- Have a clue about world softball

  Your universe is going to center around softball people, so it helps if you can be conversational in their language. Stay informed. Keep up with the U.S. national teams and high-level college softball. Know who the world's best players are. You don't have to obsess over this stuff, but at least have a working vocabulary.

6

YOU

BELONG

Preseason lifts and fall ball can be an extremely intimidating proposition. A lot of very good rookies crumble, and not because they lack talent. They crumble because they can't get their heads right. They're so worried about disappointing their coach or pissing off their teammates that they never figure out how to present their best selves. They are so worried about being bad that they never get around to being good.

Listen to me: You belong! If that coach recruited you into this team, it's only because he feels you can make his team better. Make preseason a showcase of your best self. Make it a showcase of your talent and your courage and your aggressiveness. It may work out the way you like and it may not, but when preseason ends, you want to have a clear conscience about what you brought to the field every day, so don't leave anything chips on the table! Make your decision before preseason begins about the attitude that you will bring into it. You need to choose the player that your coaches and teammates will see on that field. Don't leave it up to chance; *decide* who you will be!

Will you make mistakes? Absolutely. Softball is an imperfect game and you are an imperfect person. Don't dwell on those mistakes or I promise that you'll self-destruct. Coaches don't expect you to be perfect, so don't stress. Just do your very best with *every* chance you get. That's the only way you'll leave preseason with a clear conscience.

Yes, preseason is an audition and yes, a lot of eyes will be upon you, but that's just life and it's no reason for you to crawl into a shell. Use preseason to do more than just play softball; use it to announce yourself! Use it as a platform to prove to your coaches and teammates that you are a player who deserves to be taken seriously and that yes, you do belong!

7

THE
FITNESS
TESTS

The fitness test and lifts... the most dreaded words in college softball. But since nearly every coach employs them, or parts of them, you're going to have to just accept them as a part of life and put your head down and grind them out. Embrace the idea that 6 a.m. can truly be your friend.

Physical training is important to your coach for a number of reasons. From a purely physical standpoint, fitness matters. Your physical ability says a lot about your commitment to doing what is asked of you. You are the only one responsible for your fitness and it is one of the very few softball things over which you have complete control. To trust you, your coach needs to know that you'll do the work even when no one is watching.

This may be the first chance you have to make a statement. If you have to do it, you may as well do it in a way that shows you deserve to be taken seriously. Instead of lamenting your fitness, you may as well just embrace it and use it to your advantage.

Now, since we can't make physical training go away, let's at least make it more manageable.

In April or May you'll likely receive a summer fitness packet. Some packets are very detailed and will give you a day by day plan for your summer workouts. Your coaches put a lot of time and effort into assembling that packet and they created it to help you, so my advice is to follow it to the letter. Like I said, this will be your first chance to announce yourself, so let's take advantage of it.

Here's a piece of advice, and it's one that you'll want to pay attention to, even if you're already a fitness freak: Experience the physical training and lifts *before* you get to campus. Learn them before you have to perform them in front of your new teammates. On the first day of lifts, it shouldn't look like you've never met a squat rack before.

All the returners have participated in lifts and physical training. They are prepared. You need to be prepared also. The coach will not be encouraged if on day one, you can not squat or clean with good form and appropriate weight. Learn what the minimum standards are for your team, then train to exceed them.

If your new club uses the power clean as a lifting test and asks for a minimum of forty pounds, then clean fifty. If your new club uses the squat as a lifting test with a minimum of fifty pounds, then squat sixty. Incidentally, it doesn't matter how much weight you push if your form is poor. Either your lift won't count or worse, you'll end up injuring yourself. It's important to learn the correct form from the very beginning. If your form suffers when you add weight, you're not ready to add that weight yet. Do not sacrifice proper form.

Some coaches place greater emphasis on cardio and will expect you to pass some type of running test, like a timed mile or the Yo-Yo test. I'm not saying these coaches are in the majority or that I'm one of them, I'm just saying that they're out there. If your coach happens to fall into this camp, let me give you one more way to sharpen your axe.

Every team has a player or two who excels at running the fitness tests. It'll be pretty easy to figure out who these players are by just talking to the returners. If at all possible, line up beside one of these fitness junkies and use her to pace you. Make up your mind to stay stride for stride with her, no matter how much it hurts. Hang right beside her for as long as you can and hopefully for the duration. That way, when she passes, you do too! Just remember, there's a reason she excels at this stuff; it's because she is actually fit. If you want to keep up with her, you'd better be fit also.

8

THE
COMMITMENT
TEST

I beg of you to pay attention to what you are about to read. I want to give you a sneak peek into the pyramid of urgency for a college athlete.

Right now, college softball looks like it will go on forever. You get to experience four years of it, and four years might seem like an eternity. You probably feel that you can ease your way into it until you eventually hit your stride. That complacency puts you on the bottom of the pyramid.

On the other hand, roughly eight months after you report to your first college class, your senior teammates will see their softball careers coming to an end. The thing they love to do most of all will be taken from them and they'll never be able to get it back. That means they have one last chance to shape their legacy, one last chance to accomplish everything they had hoped to accomplish as collegiate softball players. Translated, that means they have one last chance to win championships. And that means more to them than you or any other rookie can possibly imagine.

The most exciting part of college softball —the competitive season —doesn't begin until the spring semester. As of the writing, a Division I softball team is allowed just eight games during the fall semester, a Division 3 team just one.

There are also restrictions regarding the number of days your team will be allowed to practice –on the field –during the fall. That means you're going to be doing a lot of grunt work during the fall. You're going to spend a lot of time lifting weights and conditioning. It's during this fall grind that the returners will be sizing you up, making judgments about whether you will add value to their program, or whether you were a recruiting mistake.

Your attitude and performance during the fall are about your work ethic, and for the returners, particularly the seniors, your work ethic is about the *investment* you are willing to make to help *them* reach *their* goals. So, where you see a lift or practice or a fitness test, they see a commitment test. And believe me, they are paying close attention to your results. Those early morning, mid-winter lifts that start before the sun even rises; those practices in a cold, biting wind –they are just as important to your teammates as they are to you.

Do you know the saying that you never get a second chance to make a first impression? Well, the effort on day one is the first impression the returners will have of you, and if you bomb it, they'll write you off before you leave the field that day. However, if you light your workout on fire, they'll be much more inclined to take you seriously. They'll think of you as someone they can trust to help them get to where they want to be, and that will ease your path into the inner sanctum.

Do your work over the summer. Do your work when no one is there to make sure you're doing your work. Do your work when no one else is watching. That's how your teammates will know that you're committed to the cause.

Don't ever give your teammates a reason to question your fitness or your commitment. It's something you control, so own it! Please believe me when I tell you that from your teammates' point of view, the fall lifts and practices are about whether or not they can depend on you.

9

MAKE YOUR
OWN
DECISIONS

Every team has its own chemistry and interpersonal dynamics at work. When you get to college, you're going to have a natural need to get information about your teammates and coaches. The returning players will be happy to give it to you, and often times you won't even need to ask.

When this type of information is being thrust upon you, take it with a grain of salt. The player telling you something is basing what she says on her personal experiences, and those experiences will differ from one player to the next. Just because someone is the first to tell you something, that doesn't mean her opinion is indisputable. My point is this: Be wary of the player who gossips and backstabs her teammates. She has an agenda and she is trying to recruit you to her side. She hopes to slant your view on certain people before you ever have the chance to know them. It is in your own best interest to avoid being dragged into any one clique. Stay open-minded. *Don't let other people determine your relationships.*

When a player backstabs a teammate, there may be a history there that you know nothing about. When she slams the coaches, it might be because she's been unhappy with her playing time. Whatever the motive, you're better off not drinking too much of her Kool-Aid. Just politely distance yourself from her as quickly as possible.

My advice is that you don't take anything too seriously on face value. Do yourself a favor and make up your own mind about your teammates and coaches. You may end up liking them or you may not, but make those decisions on your own terms and give everyone a fair shake. Four years later you'll be happy that you did.

10

DON'T
BURN BRIDGES

This is one of those topics that you're much better off learning ahead of time.

Here's the thing about college and college softball… it might work out and it might not work out, and there are a thousand reasons why. You might not like the academics. You might not like the social life. You might end up unhappy with your playing time or the style of play. You may end up not liking some of your teammates. You might just hate the weather. And one or more of these factors may unsettle you to the point that you decide to transfer or quit.

Now obviously we both hope that this isn't the case and that you are thrilled with your college choice and that your college softball experience is exactly as you had imagined. But we're better off preparing for the worst and hoping for the best.

If you decide to transfer and continue playing college softball, make no mistake, your coach is going to be a major part of your Plan B. You're going to need a self- release that allows you to speak to other schools. Once you have a release, chances are that you're also going to need a recommendation from your coach.

The college coaching world is far smaller than you might imagine. I would bet that there isn't a college softball coach in this country who isn't, at the very least, the friend of a friend of mine. If I don't know this coach myself, I know someone who does. Yes, we have a bubble of our very own.

When a player from another university contacts us about transferring to our university, the very first thing we do is call her coach and ask why the player is leaving. Usually the reason is perfectly valid and there are no underlying issues and it's an easy decision. Sometimes the reasons are a little more disconcerting. The important thing for you to remember is that your coach will be brutally honest. She has to be, because in our bubble, what comes around goes around. We may be competitors, but we cooperate in these situations because we have to protect our names and because eventually the shoe will be on the other foot and it will be that coach calling me about a player. My point is that your coach won't lie for you. Your coach won't make you sound better than you are. Your coach won't sugarcoat your abilities or the effect you've had on team chemistry. And, if the situation so warrants, your coach won't hesitate from telling us that you're a jerk.

The bottom line is that you need your coach, so even if you don't hit it off, do your best to maintain a positive relationship. If you're unhappy, don't go around lighting fires because you'll only end up burning yourself. Minimize your losses so if the time to transfer rolls around, your coach will be inclined to say nice things about you.

If you should decide to transfer, I strongly suggest that you inform your coach immediately once your season has ended. Your coach will want as much time as possible to replace you, particularly if you are a starter or on scholarship. Your coach might not like that you're leaving, but she will appreciate the early notice because it gives her the best chance to find another player. When it comes to recruiting, every day matters. If you wait until mid-May to announce your intentions, you've left your coach with very little opportunity to find your replacement and she might not think so highly of you. And that's not the person you want talking to other coaches on your behalf.

If you decide to leave, keep this in mind: At the moment that you communicate your decision, you basically cease to exist as a softball player at your university. All of the resources you had at your disposal a day earlier will vanish. You won't be allowed to attend training sessions. You'll be cut off from the weight room. You won't even have access to a batting helmet. Now none of that should stop you from making a decision that is in your best long-term interest; I just want you to be emotionally prepared if you decide to take that leap.

11

YOUR

SHOPPING LIST

You're going to think of plenty of things to bring with you to the first fall and fall workouts at your university! Excellent! Your room should be an oasis of self-sufficiency, and that takes preparation. When you've got a busy schedule, you don't want to have to run to the store to buy something you forgot. Let me give you a few things that probably haven't made your list but should.

Shoelaces –Everyone's shoelaces break somewhere along the line and it's never at a good time. If your laces snap when you're tying up your cleats for the evening scrimmage, you don't want to spend 30 minutes trying to find a replacement while the game goes on without you. Carry a spare pair in the same color in your softball bag. As a matter of fact, carry two. Then you'll be able to help out a friend. Just make sure you buy the proper color.

Febreze –Be a citizen. Spray down your bat bag and batting gloves with Febreze to keep your room from smelling like a zoo. We had a player whose cleats smelled fine, but her batting gloves brought tears to the dugout.

Dr. Scholl's Odor X Spray –It's Febreze for your feet! Spray it on your feet to keep them healthy and spray it inside your cleats to keep them from stinking up your entire locker room.

A&D Ointment / Zinc Oxide Cream –There's an exceptionally high likelihood that you're going to experience a physical discomfort that I will politely refer to as *swamp butt*. And nothing is more irritating than a good old-fashioned case of swamp butt. A&D Ointment and Zinc Oxide Cream will get you back to normal pretty quickly, and you'll be very thankful that you brought them along.

Toilet Paper –When you have a case of swamp butt, that's not the time you want to discover that the dormitory toilet paper isn't quite as fluffy as you like. Bring a few rolls of your personal favorites just in case.

Cooler –You're going to need ice at all hours of the day and night. A cooler on hand will save you the trouble of hauling yourself out of your room or out of your building to reload your ice bags.

Ace Bandages –Use them to tie your ice packs to your body.

Pre-wrap –Because of its many functions, pre-wrap is like duct tape for softball players.

Sun Block –You'll be outside. Protect yourself. You've got enough to worry about; you don't need a sunburn.

Aloe –For those times when you forgot to apply your sun block. Keep it in your dorm fridge for maximum relief.

Lip Protection –You're going to be doing a lot of breathing through your mouth which can lead to a severe case of chapped lips. No fun.

Bug Spray –Nothing disappears faster than bug spray. Keep a can stashed away in your bag for those times when the trainer's supply runs out.

Newspaper –When your cleats are wet, the best way to dry them out is to stuff them with balls of newspaper. The problem is usually finding the newspaper. Bring some along with you and you'll be one step ahead of the game.

Two Alarm Clocks –That's right, two. As in plural. Why? Well, for starters, one might not do the trick. More importantly, if one fails, you have a back-up. Keep your alarm clock several feet from the bed. This will force you to get out of bed to shut that sucker off. Once you get to your feet, you're much less likely to fall back asleep.

SECTION 2

MEET
YOUR COACH

12

MEET YOUR
COACH

Meet your college softball coach. He is not your club coach or your high school coach. This team is not something he does on the side to supplement the income of his *real* job. He has a mortgage and a car payment, a wife, 2.5 kids and a dog. All of them depend on him to pay the bills and put food on the table. This isn't his hobby. Everything he does is centered on this one team. All of his energy is devoted to making this one team the best that it can possibly be.

His view of college softball is much different than yours. Where you see the glory and the crowds and your picture on the website; he sees the paycheck he can't afford to lose. If you want to know why your coach gets pissed when you are thirty seconds late to a meeting, it's because he sees the big picture and knows that the little things matter.

Your coach has a job and he wants to keep it. To keep his job, the one thing he absolutely must do is win softball games. His fate is inextricably tied to the performance of a group of teenagers. Reread that last sentence ten years from now and you'll appreciate both the humor and agony.

Meet your coach. She serves many masters. In addition to the family that depends on her for survival, she serves a university that depends on her to set a good example; to play by the rules; to behave ethically; and to graduate players. And yes, this university depends on her to win games.

Meet your coach. She serves many masters and you aren't one of them. She'll do her best to look after you, to provide you with guidance and to keep you safe. She wants what's best for you, but not at the expense of what's best for herself and her program. She has other masters.

Meet your coach. There will be days when you think your coach is an idiot. Rest assured, sometimes she feels the same way about you.

Meet your coach. He would love it if his team won *and* you were happy, but if he must choose just one, well, you're out of luck. Remember, he has other masters, and the university really doesn't care if you're unhappy with your playing time. He is going to make his decisions based on one very simple premise: *What is in the best interest of my program?* You might not always enjoy his answer.

Meet your coach. She genuinely likes you and cares about you. She wants to see you do well. She'll do her best to treat you fairly and to help you up when you fall. She'll consider you family. She'll be sad when your career is over and proud on the day you graduate. But remember, this is not a one-way street. You are expected to hold up your end of the deal. You are a direct reflection of your coach in the eyes of her many masters.

Meet your coach. There will be many days when you are convinced that you know better than she does. You do not.

Meet your coach. He will likely be the only college softball head coach you ever have. To you, he will always be one of one. To your coach, you are one of many; one of many who want more from him —more of his time, more of his approval, more of his attention.

Meet your coach. In four years, you're going to ask her to write a letter of recommendation.

Meet your coach. No matter what you think of him, he is the one person you must please to get on the field.

13

YOUR
RELATIONSHIP

You're going to have some type of relationship with your coach, whether that relationship is close, distant or something in between. Regardless of the distance, you obviously want to have a positive relationship with the coach, so you can start by not making her life any more difficult than it already is. We'll go into some specifics later, but for now let me suggest that you strive to be someone that your coach will refer to as *high-trust, low-maintenance*. If you exist as a hard-working, responsible and dependable person who doesn't drag drama into her life, your coach is going to like you, a lot.

Some players want to have a close relationship with their coach, some do not. It's completely your choice and either way is fine. You don't have to have a close relationship to have a positive one. You'll get to know your coach and your coach will get to know you just because you'll spend so much time together. I've genuinely liked plenty of players I wasn't necessarily close with, and I would imagine every other coach would say the same.

But some players want more from their relationship; some players were close with their club or high school coach and they want the same type of relationship with their college coach, or they want the college coach to serve as a parental figure.

You can have whatever type of relationship you choose, however, understand that your relationship with your coach is up to you, not her. If you are a player that wants to be close with the coach, you'll be more than welcomed to do that, but *you* have to be the catalyst in that relationship. Keep in mind that *close* is a relative term and there are some lines that can't be crossed, and each coach determines those lines for themselves. Some coaches insist on being called by their first name, while others won't answer to anything but 'Coach.' Some coaches will invite you to their house for dinner. Others insist that you don't call them after office hours unless there's an emergency. Remember, your coach has other masters and you are not always the primary concern.

There are a lot of eyes on your coach, and her objectivity needs to remain above reproach. Let's translate that to mean that your coach doesn't want people to think that playing time preference is given to the players she likes more than others. That means no matter how much your coach enjoys your sparkling personality, she can't actively seek out a relationship with you. If you want a close relationship, you'll have to go make one. Thankfully it's really quite simple.

If you want a relationship that goes deeper than Xs and Os, then you're asking that your coach see you as more than just a player. For that to happen, you need to see her as more than just a coach. That's a difficult proposition if your only interactions are on the softball field. To strengthen your relationship, start by doing some things that don't involve a ball and cleats, like popping by her office once in a while to chat about whatever is on your mind, and that shouldn't be limited to softball. Let your coach get to know you on a personal level and she may let you do the same.

When there's a team meal, don't be afraid to sit with the coaches if the seating arrangement allows. Most players try to physically distance themselves from their coaches at meals, and that's fine, too. But if the seating arrangement dictates that the coaches and players will share a table, pick a seat near the coach. The conversation at team meals usually doesn't revolve around softball, so these meals provide an excellent chance for you to get to know your coach, and for her to get to know you.

There are countless opportunities for you to connect with your coach. Bus rides, hotel lobbies, fundraisers, community service, clinics and other non-softball events all offer you a chance to build that relationship. But it's up to you to take the relationship to her.

Much like the whole of your college softball experience, when it comes to your relationship with your coach, you'll get out of it what you put into it.

14

SLIPPERY SLOPE

As you ponder the type of relationship you want to have with your coach, please heed this bit of warning: *Don't base your relationship on playing time.*

Remember when we said that you want your coach to see you as more than just a player? Well, that won't be possible if you base your relationship on how many innings you get on the field, or where you fall in the batting order. If you are going to be friendly when you play and antisocial when you don't, you'll never win your coach's respect. For your coach to value you as more than just a player, you'll have to value him as more than just a coach. That means you can't base your entire relationship on game-day decisions about who plays where and for how long. If playing time is going to be the foundation for how you judge your coach, he is going to distance himself from you in a hurry. To have a positive relationship with your coach, you need to keep playing-time in its own compartment.

15

GOOD COP,
BAD COP

At some point during your college softball career, there's a reasonable chance that you're going to wish that the assistant coach was actually the head coach. This isn't uncommon and I'll tell you why.

On most coaching staffs there is a good cop, bad cop dynamic. As the players see it, the head coach is the bad cop. (But I really tried not to be the bad cop). The assistant coach is the good cop. Or Santa Claus. And everyone likes Santa Claus more than they like the bad cop.

At many programs, the assistant is the coach the players feel comfortable approaching with their issues. She serves as a sounding board to the players and an intermediary to the head coach. Her role as a go-between is vital in ensuring that the players have a voice in the program. The players understand this and they like her for it. Plus, the assistant is usually younger, cooler, and better looking.

The big reason that the assistant coach always wins the popularity contest is that she doesn't have to make any of the truly difficult and impactful decisions. She has the luxury of being closer to the players because her objectivity isn't tested nearly as much as her boss'. The head coach needs to keep players at arm's length because there can't be personal feelings interfering with the ability to make the difficult decisions that best serve the program. And ultimately, all of the tough calls fall to the person at the top.

When I say that the head coach is the bad cop, I'm not implying that she is inherently mean, impolite, unlikeable, humorless, or incapable of compassion. I'm just saying that a college softball program is a business, and the head coach is the CEO. There are decisions that need to be made that are in the company's best interest and those decisions aren't always easy and they aren't always popular.

It is the head coach who determines playing time, and that, in and of itself, will send some players campaigning for the assistant. The head coach also decides who gets scholarship money and who doesn't and what player gets more scholarship money than her roommate. The head coach decides who gets cut and just as importantly, whose best friend gets cut. If a punishment is doled out, it's the head coach doing the doling. This is no way to win a popularity contest.

These unpleasant tasks are all good and necessary to build a strong program, which is why the good cop, bad cop dynamic isn't such a horrible thing. Having a head coach that keeps a safe distance is good for you because it helps ensure that decisions will be objective and fair and, in the team's best interest. My point is this: Just because your head coach keeps you at a safe distance, it doesn't mean she doesn't like you or care about you. She probably likes you more than you think. And believe me, if the assistant coach became the head coach, her days as the popularity contest winner would be numbered too.

16

CHOOSE YOUR
COACH

Your college coach doesn't want to compete with other coaches for your undivided attention. The day you leave for college is the day you need to jettison your other coaches, and that may include your parents. Now I'm not suggesting that you completely eradicate them from your life, but you do need to eradicate them as your softball advisors.

You're graduating into a whole new softball life. To get on the field in this new life, there is only one person you need to please and that person is your head coach. The coach may want you to play a certain way and will explain these expectations to you. It is up to you to rise up and meet them. It really is that simple.

Your former coaches may not agree with your new coach's philosophies or how he utilizes you or how much playing time he gives you, but none of that matters anymore because they don't run your new team. And any advice they offer that contradicts your new coach is detrimental to your chances of playing and developing as an important part of your new team.

Imagine you had to run a 50-yard dash against seven other competitors, but you had to wear a forty-pound backpack and the other runners didn't. That's what happens when you hang on to your previous coaches: They weigh you down and the other competitors pass you by. Now, imagine how much faster you would run if you got rid of that backpack. That's what happens when you release yourself from your former coaches.

You can only have one head coach. When you listen to voices that conflict with his, you are hurting your own chances to get on the field. You need to choose your head coach and say goodbye to the others.

If you're one of those players who can't let go of your previous coaches, you're going to struggle. Do yourself a favor and make a clean break.

17

YOUR COACH IS
NOT PSYCHIC

Don't expect your coach to know the things that you don't tell her.

If you show up to practice in a funk and that negatively affects the way you're playing, there's a pretty good chance you're going to hear about it from your coach. Why? Because that's part of her job. Don't expect her to know that the reason you're in a funk is because you bombed an exam or that your boyfriend is being a pinhead.

You are expected to live up to certain expectations. If there are mitigating circumstances that will compromise your ability to meet those expectations, then get out in front of the issue and let the coach know what's affecting you; otherwise she is just going to assume that your level of effort or concentration is substandard, and at that point you've dug yourself a hole. You are an adult now, so your coach is going to assume that when you need help, you'll ask for it.

We had signed an awesome, first-year first baseman, who I'll call Jen. Sadly, Jen's step-dad passed away shortly before her first semester in college. The two were very close, so naturally it was a tremendous loss. Understanding the precariousness of her situation, I knew this kid was going to need plenty of support. I also knew that the type of support I could offer would only go so far and that it would be a good idea to get a qualified counselor involved. I asked numerous times if Jen would like to speak to a professional, but she always assured me that she was fine.

On her first Friday night as a college student, Jen did what a lot of first-years do. She went out and drank way too much. Making a bad situation significantly worse, that night Jen was sexually assaulted. She told no one, but the emotional pain was immense.

Alcohol became Jen's coping mechanism. She began drinking more. She became defiant. She came to practice under the influence. She was a train wreck and I had no idea why. I assumed it had to do with the loss of her step-father, but I had severely underestimated the weight this kid had been carrying around. Whenever I broached the topic with her, Jen refused to open up, and she refused to see a counselor. At my wit's end, I threatened to remove her from the team.

Then one Sunday night, our team captain called me in a panic. Jen had finally told someone something. The three of us met in my office at 9 p.m., and Jen laid it all out on the table. I was stunned at how little I knew about what she was enduring. I was thankful that Jen was finally opening up, sad that she hadn't felt comfortable coming to me sooner, and mortified that I had come so close to cutting her. There was so much going on in her life that I was completely blind to. Thankfully, in one of those *better late than never* moments, we were able to rally around her, get her the help she needed, and help her craft a happy ending.

Jen played all four years, was an all-everything player, and is a dear friend of my family. She has a wonderful career in engineering and volunteers to speak to athletes about the importance of seeking help when help is what's needed. In short, she is living her best life. I am so happy, and so relieved, that I didn't release Jen from our team. I couldn't possibly be prouder of who this young woman has become.

Your coach may be a lot of things, but she certainly isn't psychic. If you have a problem that your coach might need to know about, say so. You can't expect her to know what's going on in your life if you don't actually share what's going on in your life. Coaches are programmed to help. Give your coach that chance.

18

MIND YOUR PRONOUNS

Let's do a little exercise in translation.

When a player says: "A lot of the players think that…"
The coach hears: "Me and my roommate think that…"

When a player says: "We all would like to…"
The coach hears: "I would like to… (and I hope some of my teammates feel the same way)."

When you approach your coach to speak about an issue, speak on your own behalf. Casually expanding your pronouns won't camouflage your agenda. Be an adult and say what you need to say. Have the conviction to present your case on its own merits instead of trying to fluff it up with support from phantom teammates.

I don't imagine you'll approach your coach very often as a rookie, but this advice will serve you well throughout your career.

Say what you mean and mean what you say.

19

BE ON TIME

If you want to announce your predilection for irresponsibility, show up late for team functions.

I don't know who first said that *on time means early*, but I'll bet it was a coach. Coaches are fanatics about getting things started on time. Ask anyone who has ever played for us. Lateness makes coaches crazy. You need to know this going in.

Your coach has a limited amount of your time, so everything needs to run on schedule. He is also in charge of the team culture, so it's important that players show respect for the time of their teammates. When the coach says we'll meet at 10 a.m., he expects everyone to be in their places by 9:55 a.m.

When players are late, usually it's only by a minute or two. The reason players end up a minute or two late is because they didn't leave themselves enough margin for error. If they were supposed to be somewhere at 10 a.m., they tried to time it so they would walk through the door at 9:55. They didn't anticipate hitting every red light, or the accident that was blocking a lane of traffic, or that the hotel elevator would stop at every floor on the way to the lobby. When they encounter one of these surprises, all of the sudden their plan falls apart and they are late and the coach is unhappy.

Being responsible means being on time. You've got to allow for the possibility of unexpected delays and factor them into your plan. It does a coach's heart good to see his team against the wall at 5:50 a.m. for a 6 a.m. lift. Granted the players may have their eyes shut, but hey, they're on time. Show up five minutes late or, worse, no-show because you overslept, and you have a problem. And that's when you'll wish you paid more attention to the two alarm-clocks rule.

If I'm scheduled to meet with the Athletic Director at 10 a.m., you can bet I'm going to be sitting in his lobby by 9:50 a.m. As the saying goes, *better an hour early than a minute late.*

I could find a thousand different ways to explain to you why it's important that you show up on time, or you can just trust me that it is. How about you just trust me on this one?

Incidentally, if you are going to be late, call the coach yourself. Don't ask your teammate to deliver the news because that just won't fly. Ever.

20

DELIVER
BAD NEWS

Somewhere along the line there's a chance that you'll stumble into some real trouble. I hope that's not the case, but life happens. Whether that trouble involves your R.A. or your biology professor or the local police force, rest assured that your coach will find out. Remember that bubble we talked about? Yeah, she's going to find out.

In these moments, one of the scariest things you will have to do is tell your coach. Do it anyway and do it right away. Here's why:

First of all, your coach hates surprises. When it comes to problems of significant magnitude, your coach's boss, the Athletic Director, is going to end up being involved. Your coach wants the chance to tell the A.D. before the A.D. tells her. The coach wants the chance to say, "We've had this problem, I felt you should know, and this is how I plan on handling it." It shows the A.D. that the coach hasn't lost control of her program, and that's a big deal. When the A.D. knows about these things before the coach does, the coach looks less than professional and doesn't appreciate the person who made her look that way.

Bringing the news to your coach also gives you a chance to control the story before all of the rumors start swirling around. There comes a time and a place to put all your cards on the table and just confess your sins. This is that time and place.

Finally, and this is important, you've got to give the coach a chance to help you. When you go into your coach's office and unload your story, yeah, you'll probably have to face some consequences. But you know what, you'll survive them. What's far more important is that you give your coach a chance to be your ally so that you can face this difficult time together. If you don't recruit your coach as your ally, then she may be left with no choice but to cut her losses and desert you. No matter what the problem is, you're much better off having the coach on your side, so get her involved sooner rather than later.

Coaches are programmed to take care of their players. You've got to give your coach that chance. When you go to her first and accept responsibility for your mistakes, it shows that you are putting your trust in her to take care of you, and that's going to help your cause.

It's difficult for someone your age to understand how much a coach values being first in the loop. Being informed is a reflection of her professionalism. And whatever problem you're facing, it's likely something she's dealt with before. Over the years, my players have found a myriad of ways to color outside of the lines. They've been written up for playing their music too loudly, for hanging flashing lights on their doors, and one player got tagged for keeping a cat in her room. Each time, in the moment, it was a major deal to the player, but a minor deal to me and we sorted things out.

21

NEVER LIE

When you report for your first season, you have several unblemished character traits, and one of them is your credibility. It will behoove you greatly to protect it.

Here's the thing... when you lie to your coach, you may solve a short-term problem. But if he ever finds out that you lied, your credibility is annihilated. And the chances of him finding out are excellent, *even if he never actually tells you that he found out.* Remember that you'll be living in a bubble, and word travels through that bubble with breakneck speed, particularly when a student-athlete is involved. For whatever reason, people *love* telling coaches about their misbehaving players.

Incidentally, word doesn't necessarily need to make it back to your coach for him to know that you're lying. Despite what you think, your coaches aren't idiots. They were once college students themselves and, as hard as this might be for you to believe, they still have pretty clear memories of those days. They know the types of situations you can get yourself into and they know the lies you might tell to save yourself. Most of the time they'll see right through your BS.

When you're sitting in the coach's office and the conversation is a tense one, I beg of you to tell the truth. At some point during that conversation, your coach is going to ask you a question about a possible indiscretion that you were a part of or aware of. Believe me when I tell you that he almost certainly knows the answer before the question is asked. The question is just testing you. And if you fail that test once, you've failed it forever.

Since the day you were brought into this world your parents have been telling you not to lie. That's not by accident. They understand that the short-term consequence of telling the truth outweighs the long-term consequence of lying. You should take their advice.

22

SAY
THANK YOU

If you want to get college coaches into a frenzied conversation, mention the word *entitlement*. Coaches have a surplus of stories about players who feel they are entitled to everything they've been given and who keep asking for more. A disproportionate amount of what a coach hears can be translated to *gimme, gimme, gimme*. Believe me, it's exhausting.

Every coach enjoys a player that shows some appreciation for all that she is given. Show that these gestures and perks don't go unnoticed by occasionally saying thank you. Your coach will appreciate it and her opinion of you will rise.

SECTION 3

PRESEASON

23

IT'S A JOB

"People don't play sports because it's fun. Ask any athlete; most of them hate it, but they couldn't imagine their life without it. It's part of them —the love/hate relationship. It's what they live for. They live for the practices, parties, cheers, long bus rides, invitationals, countless pairs of different types of shoes, water, Gatorade, and coaches you hate but appreciate. They live for the way it feels when they beat the other team, and knowing those two extra sprints they ran in practice were worth it. They live for the way they become a family with their team. They live for the countless songs they sing in their head while training all those hours. They live for the competition. They live for the friends, the practices, the memories, the pain. It's who they are. It's who we are."

– Anonymous*

Make no mistake about it; college softball is a job. That will never be more clear than at 6 a.m. on an early September morning when you hear the alarm you could swear you set just five minutes earlier. As you roll over to silence that alarm, you'll feel a pain in your legs like nothing you've ever known, like a load of bricks has fallen upon them from three stories above. Your back and neck will be so stiff that you'll hear the vertebrae snap into place like ice cubes being twisted from their tray. You'll barely have the strength in your arm to reach that clock. You won't want to get up. The voice in your head will try coaxing you back into that beautiful sleep. It will tell you how much happier you will be if you just stay in bed. It will say, *Just lay here for five more minutes. Trust me. You won't fall back asleep.*

No, you won't want to get up. But you will anyway. Why? Because this is your job now, and as painful as it might be, you know that it is the greatest job you'll ever have and you refuse to give it up just to stay under the covers. Welcome to fall ball. Day Two.

College softball will be much more demanding of your time than club or high school softball ever was. In addition to your field practices, there are team meetings and early morning lifts. There are tutors and study halls. When you sign up to play college softball, you are making a tremendous commitment, and at times this commitment can feel downright overwhelming. More than anything, it is this time commitment that leads us to define college softball as a job. And soon, you'll understand the weight of that commitment.

How you position preseason is important. If you think of it as a few weeks of job prep for the spring season, that's exactly what it will be, so let me give you a more useful outlook. Fall ball is the closest thing to a professional job interview, so get prepared and get positive!

Think of fall ball as your showcase. You've spent months preparing; the fall is your chance to show everyone how hard you've worked while no one was watching. It's your chance to announce yourself as someone who has made the physical investment and is committed to bringing success to the program. It is your chance to show your coaches that you are a player who deserves to be taken seriously!

Is that going to make it hurt any less? A little bit. Maybe. Okay, fall ball may hurt either way, but as the saying goes, *Pain is inevitable; suffering is optional.*

Do yourself a favor and have a plan for how you will approach each day of fall ball physically and mentally. Predetermine the mentality you will bring to the field each day, even when your body is crying out for relief. It won't hurt like this forever. Make a decision about the player and person you will be, even when it hurts. Make a plan to be your very best self and then remember to stick to it.

I stumbled upon this quote online, and no one seems to know where exactly it came from.

24

BIGGER POND,
BIGGER FISH

I was a college soccer player who became a college soccer coach who then fell into being a college softball coach. I became a softball coach for precisely two reasons: One, I played and loved baseball. And two, I was standing in the hallway in January of 1981 as a soccer coach, when the Athletic Director announced the softball coach had left. Could I fill in? You bet! Let's face it, I was young and needed the money. Turns out we played very well, I enjoyed the experience and never looked back.

My first college preseason was a long time ago, so most of the details have gone fuzzy. I do remember as a freshman soccer player at a large university, we had been told all players would need to run a 5:30 mile. Those that did not would be sent home. Period. I trained all summer and on test day, I ran a 5:28 mile. I played college soccer for four years, but a lot of players went home that day. Right or wrong, that was the first rule I learned: Listen to the rules.

There is however, another moment that I recall vividly. It was the day we were handed our match schedule for the season. I don't remember that schedule because of the new opponents I was about to face, or because of the dates and times and locations of the games. Everything that I remember about that piece of paper was typed right there on the first line:
Men's Soccer Schedule.

I had been playing soccer since the age of thirteen and playing for my school since the ninth grade, and in all those years of school and club ball, my greatest passion and the thing I could never get enough of was always referred to as "Boys' Soccer." And now, this piece of paper delivered the news that I would never again play a game of boys' soccer. Now I was playing as a man.

When you were U-12, you played U-12 softball. When you were U-18, you played U-18 softball. The instant you step onto the college softball field, you've just graduated to U-23 softball. That's a gigantic leap! Everything you know about softball is about to get bigger and faster and more physical.

There's a competitive pyramid of softball. The bottom of the pyramid is based solely on participation and is crowded with very young, recreational players. As you got older, you moved up the pyramid and with each step of your climb, the pyramid got less crowded as fewer players kept climbing. Now, as you begin college softball, you're very close to the point of that pyramid. Not many players make it to this level. The ones that do have shown some grit, some gift of talent and athleticism and the ability to adapt to the new challenges offered at each new step of the climb. You are one of those players! So are your teammates. You didn't get here by accident. And neither did they.

Meet your college softball teammates. Every one of them was the best player at her high school or on her club. Yet some of them won't make it on the field.

You were a big fish in your last pond, but your new pond is much bigger, and so are the fish. Now you get to swim with the man-eaters.

You'll probably take some lumps in preseason. Things that worked really well for you against high school-aged players might not work as well against a 22-year-old senior. It's okay. Don't freak out and don't keep banging your head against the same wall. The way to survive in your new pond is to simply keep doing your best and adapting to the new demands.

Your teammates won't lie down for you. They aren't there just to make you look good. They're fighting to make a favorable impression on the coach... so are you! They're fighting for playing time... so are you! This time the fight is just going to be a little more difficult.

Remember, you belong here. Do your best. Don't ever quit. Fight like hell. This is your proving ground and everything you've ever done in your softball life has led you to this moment. Stand up and make a case for yourself.

25

YOUR
BEST SELF

The first season of the television show *Survivor* was won by a corporate consultant named Richard Hatch. Among his many claims to fame (or infamy), Hatch was the mastermind of *Survivor's* very first contestant alliance. He was reviled by the television audience for his willingness to manipulate the other contestants, but in the end, his deviousness was proven to be quite practical and it won him the million-dollar grand prize.

There was one clear difference that separated Hatch from the other contestants: Hatch went into *Survivor* with a plan. As a matter of fact, Hatch himself said he was amazed that, with a million dollars on the line, no one else had bothered to devise a strategy to win the game. While the other contestants were trying to figure things out on the fly, Hatch's plan kept him two steps ahead of them from start to finish.

If fall ball is going to be your showcase, then you obviously need to showcase your very best self. It is my firm belief that, much like Richard Hatch, you are far better served by planning for the fall than by just showing up and trying to adjust on the fly.

Incidentally, I am not suggesting that you employ the same types of underhanded tactics that Richard Hatch utilized. As a matter of fact, I strongly advise you against tactics of manipulation because they will be counterproductive and your membership on your team will be short-lived. You are part of a team, whereas *Survivor* was the essence of *every man for himself*. That's a big, big difference. I only mention the *Survivor* reference because of its parallels to a college fall season, namely, a lot of people competing in a game, under difficult conditions, for a big prize and almost none of them having any clear-cut plan.

Since the fall season is going to have such a big impact on your softball life, it's worth taking the time to formulate a plan. My advice is that you enter into a contract with yourself. If your fall season is four weeks long plus twelve weeks of lifting, then that is the duration of your contract. Write out this contract several days before you leave for college. This contract is your plan and your commitment to showcasing your best self. I'm even going to provide you with the clauses of your contract.

- Train like a pro.
  As we've discussed, college softball can be exhausting. Doesn't matter. Remember this line from Alistair Cooke: *A professional does her best even when she doesn't feel like it.* You get to choose how you will approach each segment of each training season. Choose a great attitude.

- Under-promise and over-deliver.
  Don't burden yourself with additional expectations by announcing what you're going to do. Be humble. Be modest. Then go out and shock everyone.

- Outwork everyone, every day.
  This is the closest thing I can offer to a magic formula for earning playing time. If you are genuinely the hardest worker on a daily basis, your coach is going to find a spot for you. Like anything else, this won't happen by accident. If you want to be the hardest worker, then plan to be the hardest worker.

- Don't complain.
  Fall practice is a wonderful breeding ground for complaints. It's hot or cold. Of course, it is. It's the fall! What did you expect? Your legs may hurt. Your arms may hurt. You're working hard. What did you expect? When you focus on the things that bother you, you begin to lose focus on the things that matter most. Don't waste your energy focusing on the things you can't control. The more you focus on them, the more they will consume you. Let your teammates do the complaining. The coaches will notice that you're staying above it.

- Be durable.
  There's a difference between pain and injury and your ability to tell them apart can keep you on the field. Coaches know that training is painful for everyone. They notice and appreciate the players with the intestinal fortitude to tough it out. You will notice that many of your teammates will sit out some sessions with *injuries*. Don't worry too much about them. You see, there's a great healing miracle that occurs every preseason: On the day before the first game or scrimmage, everyone is magically healthy again. Use preseason to show off your toughness and durability. You won't win a position by sitting on the trainer's table or in the dugout. As a wise person once said, your best ability is availability.

- Touch the line.
  Be the type of athlete that you would admire. Whatever misery you must endure, attack it! Don't cut corners because that will just devalue your investment. Your first fall lasts only lasts for about ten weeks, so you will survive. Give your best to it every step of the way. When the coach calls for a water break, jog off the field. When the water break is over, jog back on. When the coach calls everyone together in the middle of the field, don't walk toward the coach; run! And when you are running gassers, touch the line with every single repetition. Why? Because that's what your best self would do.

- Use the fatigue of your teammates.
  All of your teammates will be fatigued. There will be at least one session where the team moves about as well as zombie herd. This is a tremendous opportunity for you. When everyone else's level is going down, make yours go up. No matter how bad it hurts, force yourself to raise your level and you'll shine brighter than a diamond.

- Be low-maintenance.
  Don't reveal yourself as someone who needs to have a babysitter. Remember your equipment. Turn off your phone before team meetings. Get to everything on time. And for heaven's sake, take care of your injuries! When you get to college, treatment is not optional.

- Don't Coach.
  No one wants to be corrected by a rookie. There is nothing more annoying than a rookie who wants to coach her teammates. Your job is to do your best, not to worry about the hitting technique of your teammates. Communicate and compete, but don't coach.

Okay, so now you have some solid and practical ideas that you can use to establish your contract. If you polled all of the college softball coaches in the country, I would bet that every one of them would tell you that what you just read is excellent advice.

Don't let preseason just happen to you. Have a plan in place and attack it!

26

ADAPT

The fall isn't necessarily just about the best players coming into the fall workouts; it's also about the players who adapt best to the new demands of the college game. Many high-profile recruits have been leapfrogged by a lesser-known player who did a better job of adjusting her game to meet the needs of her new team and coach.

Coaches want to get their best players on the field because, let's face it, it gives us the best chance of winning. But sometimes we end up with a stockpile of talented players at a single position. It's a lot more efficient to move a more-talented player to a new position than it is to wait for a less-talented player to develop at that same spot.

Versatile softball players are gems and stand an excellent chance of finding their way onto the field. My Widener team once had five shortstops on the field. The best shortstop played shortstop, then we put one at second base, one at third, and two more in the outfield. Those last two had never played outfield, but they were awesome athletes and darn good hitters. That was one of the best defensive teams I ever coached, all because those players were willing to adapt to get themselves on the field.

Be prepared to change your position. You may have played first your entire life. Your college coach may realize that you would make a fine third baseman. If that's the case, jump at the chance! You'll be much happier playing third than watching as the understudy at first. Your job is to get yourself on the field. If that means changing positions, so be it!

A new coach means new rules and new expectations. Don't hang onto your old ideals at the expense of your playing time. Decide to be flexible and willing to adapt to your new environment. The sooner you adapt to these new expectations, the sooner you'll get on the field.

27

THE

SOCIAL CONTRACT

When you join a team, you agree to accept correction from the coach.* That is the social contract that you enter, and believe me, it is binding. Your coach has a responsibility to demand the best from you, and your coach can't do that silently. Everyone gets correction. Even you.

One of the best favors you can do for yourself is to be coachable. When the coach corrects you, your coach feels they are helping you and that some part of you should be grateful for having received this new nugget of wisdom. Coaching corrections are not personal attacks, so don't take them as an attempt to embarrass you in front of your peers. Your skin needs to be thicker than that.

When your coach is offering you correction, do not interrupt to say, "I know, I know." Seriously, all coaches hate that. And his response is going to be, "Well if you know it, why didn't you do it?" And that actually will be embarrassing.

When your coach is correcting you, for the love of all things Holy, do not roll your eyes! That eye roll conveys the message that you already know it all and that the coach is wasting your time when there are far better things you could be doing with your life. Now, how do you think that will go over?

Listen please… correction is a good thing. Accept it and grow from it. When your coach stops correcting you, your coach has stopped coaching you. When your coach stops coaching you, *that's the time to worry*… because your replacement is on the way.

* This phrase is from Bruce Brown, the amazing founder of Proactive Coaching. www.proactivecoaching.info

28

R*E*S*P*E*C*T

So far, I've tried to give you the best possible chance of positioning yourself for a successful first year of college softball that will hopefully lead to playing time and acceptance into your team. However, there is still one very large hurdle you have to navigate. To get a spot on the field, you're going to have to win it. That means you're going to have to compete and compete hard against your new teammates, including the returners. And that is where a good many rookies lose the plot.

There's no way around it; fall is an awkward way to kick off your college career. In its strange dichotomy, the fall softball season demands that you simultaneously cooperate with the same people you are competing against. You are locked into a mutual dependence. You have a responsibility to help one another, even while you are perhaps fighting for the same position. This can be a confusing time for a rookie, especially if you haven't yet figured out exactly what you want from your first year of college softball.

Let me simplify this conundrum for you. Before you get to the fall workouts, you've got to make a choice. You've got to decide what's more important: getting on the field or winning a popularity contest. If your top priority is to not offend your new teammates, plan on spending a lot of time watching college softball.

Yes, you will spend a large chunk of fall trying to make your teammates look good, and you will enjoy doing that. However, there will also be moments when you have to compete against the returners head-to-head, and that's going to have a massive impact on whether or not you get on the field when the spring and the first game rolls around.

Some rookies are so scared of upsetting the returners that they never get around to showcasing their best selves. The real shame of it happens months later when they realize that they are actually better than the players who are playing in front of them. When the duels begin, you need to have a clear conscience about doing your best to conquer your teammate/opponent, even if she's got some seniority on you. Hitting a dinger off the senior pitcher in a scrimmage game will certainly get you noticed, by coaches and players too! Remember what brought you to that program in the first place. I assure you it wasn't some odd fascination with watching your friends play college softball.

The bottom line is that when it comes to playing time, your teammates are also your competitors. Now you can accept that and adjust to it, or you can leave yourself at the mercy of the returning players who have already learned that lesson. Seniority doesn't equal playing time, despite the wishes of the returning players. The best players play. Period. Welcome to the show!

If you want to play, there's only one person you need to please, and that is your coach. If you want that approval, I guarantee that you won't get it by continually deferring to the upperclassmen. You'll only get it by stepping onto the field and proving that you are the best player for the job. Accept the fact that you are going to have to fight for that position and that may mean ruffling some feathers in the process. But if you want the respect of your coaches and your teammates, you're going to have to go out there and earn it.

Softball is a massive conglomeration of individual battles. You win respect by winning those battles as often as you can by as much as you can. Your teammates should not enjoy training and playing against you. For example, if the pitchers enjoy pitching against you, you're doing something very wrong.

On the other hand, if the pitchers hate pitching to you, I'd be willing to wager that you're making a favorable impression upon your coach.

Now you don't have to take my advice. You are perfectly welcome to take the more submissive approach; just remember what you'll be giving up if you do.

There is one other really interesting tidbit that will turn this whole dynamic on its ear. It has been my experience that the rookies who come in and compete the hardest actually end up winning the popularity contest anyway. Why's that? Because they add value. You see, there's a core group of returning players that sit high up in the pecking order of your new team. When it comes to team chemistry, they steer the ship. Those core players have high ambitions for their team. They are secure in their roles as players and leaders, and because they wield so much power, they shape the team dynamic. And those players are thrilled when they see a rookie who is going to add value to their team. As for the rookies who show up timid, well, they are quickly dismissed as competitive assets. The leaders may genuinely like them as people, but they won't value them as players.

I once saw a television show where a law enforcement officer was teaching children how to react if someone attempts to kidnap them. His most memorable piece of advice was to put up your best fight before the kidnapper gets you into the car. He told the children that once the kidnapper gets you into the car, the kidnapper takes control and your chances of survival are greatly reduced.

You need to think of the last day of fall ball as the car, because that's when the transition to your competitive season begins. As the games grow nearer, the shuffling of players naturally decreases as coaches make firmer decisions about their lineups. Use the fall to put up your best fight and make your strongest case. You can make giant leaps during the first semester; after that, it gets significantly more difficult to make up big chunks of ground.

The fall semester is the hardest you will have to compete against your teammates. You're basically cramming a full season into four or five weeks. Once this time ends, everything starts to shake out and everyone will calm down and settle into their roles. Once again, my point is, make your case early. Put up your best fight when it will do you the most good. The social fallout you think you'll experience is far less than what you'll actually experience. Go out and earn their respect as someone who will help the team win. Do your very best from the very beginning or, believe me, you'll end up wishing you had.

29

PLAY
TO YOUR
STRENGTHS

I wish there was one magic formula for impressing your coach, but every coach is looking for something a little bit different, so there's no one-size-fits-all proposition. Your coach is going to have her own criteria and it might take you a little while to figure out what she is looking for. In the meantime, you've got to figure out how to make your strongest case as a player who will help the team win.

Before we move into what to do to win your coach's favor, let's talk about what not to do, and this one is in fact universal. If you want your coach to see you as an asset to the team, the one thing you absolutely cannot do is strike out looking on a regular basis. You have to show that you are aggressive at the plate and will protect the plate with two strikes. Incidentally, habitually striking out swinging won't exactly help your cause either. You have to put the ball in play. Being dependable at the plate will take you a long way in this game of ours.

You probably bring some other things to the table that you'll want the coach to notice, and the fall is the time to unveil those suckers. The best on-field advice I can give you is to play to your strengths and away from your weaknesses. As over-simplified as that may sound, each year I see rookies who fail to put their best weapons on display.

If you are fast, then you need to look for opportunities to run footraces. You need to show off your horsepower every chance you get. Capitalize on chances to leg out a grounder to short, or to stretch a single into a double, or advance on a passed ball, or steal (if you have the coach's blessing). Every time you get yourself sixty feet closer to home, that's a win. If, on the other hand, you're not so fast, then you need to find ways showcase your other strengths while showing that you are smart on the basepaths. Incidentally, being slow-ish is no excuse for not hustling. Run out those ground balls like your life depends on it!

If you are an outstanding bunter, or you have a thunderbolt for a throwing arm, you'll have plenty of preseason chances to put those skills on display. Don't save them for a rainy day! Bust out your greatest hits as early as you can. And when you have the chance during scrimmages to be the center of attention, then make the most of those opportunities.

The fall may seem like an eternity, but at some point, it actually will end. Make your best case as quickly as you possibly can. Give the coach a reason to notice you and your coach will look for ways to mold your special characteristics into the framework of the team style and system.

Do your best to play the game on your terms. Give the coach a reason to notice you and then make the adjustments she asks of you. Unveil those weapons early *–like during the fall –*and you'll undoubtedly see more playing time in the spring.

30

TELL,

DON'T ASK

At some point during the fall you will scrimmage, and because the numbers may not work out quite right, your team will have a sub and the coach will leave it up to your team to take care of its own substitutions. Your coach expects that every inning or two the sub will be rotated onto the field.

When you are the sub and it's time to get back on the field, you're going to be too scared to call a returning player off the field, so you'll opt to sub a fellow rookie out of the game. This might work once. It might work twice. But it won't go on like this forever. Eventually the rotation will dictate that you're going to have to cowgirl up and pull a returning player off the field. If you're not a naturally assertive personality, this is going to be an uncomfortable moment and a tremendous test of your courage.

The players on the field don't want to come out of the game. The returners know that because you're a rookie, you're going to be pretty intimidated, and they are going to use that against you. You'll notice them mysteriously avoiding eye contact with you. This isn't by accident. If you're going to get them off the field, they're going to make you earn it by stepping up and showing some courage.

If you softly call out to the player you're hoping to sub, she's going to pretend that she doesn't hear you then she'll run onto the field. If you politely ask her if she wants to come off the field, she will politely decline. If you ask if she needs a rest, she will tell you no.

Now, you can spend a season learning what I'm about to tell you, or you can just trust me right from the start. In these situations, *Tell! Don't ask!* Muster up a half-second's worth of courage and get the that returner out! Loudly call her name. When she looks in your direction, wave her off as you start jogging onto the field.

Will she love it? No. Will she get over it? Yes. In about four seconds. Why? Because she knows this is how the system works and she knows the system is fair. A minute later she'll be shouting at someone else to get off the field and it won't bother her one bit. It's all part of the evolution.

You won't win a spot by standing on the sidelines. Sometimes getting on the field means fighting your way onto it. If you don't want to spend your whole rookie season watching other people play, you've got to be courageous enough to sub yourself onto the field.

31

TARGETING

This is the closest thing to a secret that I can offer you about competing for a position. If you're competitive and reasonably smart, you might have eventually gotten around to figuring it out on your own. I'm just going to use this opportunity to flatten out the learning curve for you.

The fall season can seem overwhelming based solely on the large number of people fighting for positions. It's pretty common to look at the herd of twenty-three players and hope to be one of the top ten (counting a DH). That type of thinking can devour you. Instead of worrying about the group of 23, we're going to focus on just one, single teammate.

Targeting is the process of figuring out exactly who you have to beat and then using that knowledge to motivate you on a daily basis. For example, if you're a catcher, and there are three other catchers on your team, you try to figure out who is the best of the three and you focus on being better than that one player each and every day. Instead of worrying about beating out twenty-two other players or three catchers, now you're focused on outshining just one of them. It's a way to streamline your focus into bite-sized portions that are easily digested.

I want you to understand that I am not talking about anything underhanded. I'm not talking about sabotaging a teammate. I'm not talking about trying to physically damage one of your teammates or even wishing for her failure. I'm talking about using this one teammate as the measuring stick for your own efforts. Each day when you step onto the field, make it your mission to be better than that one player. Whatever she does, you do it just a little bit better. Wherever she runs, you run there faster. If she quits after ninety-nine push-ups, you make sure you get to 100. If her pop-time is 2.1, make yours 2.0. Whatever the case may be, make sure you are outdistancing her, even if it's just by one inch at a time.

Why does this work? Because it gives you a concrete model to measure yourself against. It gives you a living, breathing reason to perform at your very best each day. And it works because the player you target will have no idea that she's in your crosshairs. While she is motivating you, there's a good chance that no one is motivating her.

Since catchers don't confront one another directly during a game, your opportunities to go head-to-head are limited to other drills and exercises. Make it your mission to out-hit her, out-throw her, out-block her and outlast her. You don't have to outshine your entire roster, just that one teammate. Remember, starting a first-year won't be an issue for your coach. He wants his best catcher on the field, regardless of her seniority.

It's also good to have a second target, one to showcase your offensive prowess. We'll call her your counter-target and I'm going to tell you who she is. She's your team's best pitcher. And you want to square off with her as often as possible.

This probably sounds a little bit backwards to you, and believe me, I've seen a staggering number of players take the opposite approach. If they see they are about to be matched up against the best pitcher, they'll find a reason to switch their place in line so they can hit against a softer opponent. Let me tell you why my way is better.

First of all, you don't back into great achievements. You're not going to sneak your way into the starting lineup. It's not like the umpire is going to yell,

82

"Play ball!" to commence the opening game and then the coaches are going to look on the field and think, *'Hey, how'd she get out there?'* The Trojan Horse approach won't work in this environment, so you should abandon it before you get to campus.

Counter-targeting works for the same reason that targeting works: You have a reason to be inspired when your counter-target might not. While she'll still play hard and well *–she is the best pitcher for a reason –*you'll be playing with something just a little bit more. While she may be determined to play well, you'll be determined to beat *her*. Believe me, there's a difference. And when you demonstrate that you can hit the best pitcher, someone will notice, and that someone is your coach.

Will this always work? There's no guarantee, but if you can consistently win your battles against the best pitcher or catcher on the team, your coach is going to notice, and he's going to have a hard time keeping you off the field.

Look, you're going to be competing against these teammates countless times throughout the season anyway. You can't duck them all year. Why not just roll the dice and try your luck from the very beginning when making a statement will do you the most good? Proving that you can beat the best is an excellent way to get yourself on the field.

32

DON'T

DISQUALIFY YOURSELF

When you're fighting for playing time, whether it's in preseason or beyond, the first thing you must take care of is ensuring that you don't disqualify yourself. The difference between you and the teammate you're competing against might be almost invisible. When it's time for the coach to decide who gets the spot, it might not be about the player who pulled ahead in the race; it might be about the player who fell out of it. Don't break the tie by getting careless. Show up early, leave late, work hard all the time, hustle everything and be a pillar of positivity.

Your job is to make the coach's decision difficult. When you break team rules or negatively affect team chemistry, you make her decision very easy. You will not be rewarded for failing to live up to the team's standards. I've said it over and over and I'll continue to do so: You've got to control the things you have the power to control.

Make sure you're taking care of the little things. Again, get to team functions on time. Obey the curfews and whatever other policies are in place. Don't lie or backstab your teammates. Don't doze off during a video session. And don't commit a social media blunder. To win the race, you first have to finish the race.

There's no way for me to adequately stress the importance of not disqualifying yourself. I've seen talented players take themselves out of the equation year after year after year. It's happened on my teams, and it will also happen on yours. The good news is that you're now aware of it, so you can use it to your advantage. *Responsible behavior* will help you somewhere down the road. You'll read more about that later.

When it comes to staying in the race, don't underestimate the value of discipline. It's not just rule-breaking that can lead to your disqualification; a lapse in physical performance will have that same effect. You need to maintain your highest level of performance each and every day to stay on course to finish the race. Not all of your teammates will be able to deliver their very best on a daily basis. When their level of play drops, they fall off of the lead pack and a separation grows between them and the front-runners.

Let me put it to you another way. Think of every player on your team as a helium balloon. When you're all playing at your best, you're all bumping up against the ceiling. As a few of those balloons begin to lose some air, they begin to drop. They might not sink all the way to the floor, but they won't stay up at the same high level as the other balloons. The balloons that are up against the ceiling didn't get any higher, but because some of the other balloons sank, they look better by comparison. This is a fairly common phenomenon during the fall season. It's not always about being the player that rises higher. Sometimes it's about not being the player who sinks. And what you do *off the field* will have a tremendous impact on the amount of helium in your balloon.

College offers you all types of freedoms that high school never did, and those freedoms will begin availing themselves to you immediately. Those freedoms will suck some of your teammates down the drain, and if you're not careful, you'll go down with them.

You have a fall mission, and that mission is to prove to your coach that you belong on the field. Your climb is steep enough already. Don't make it any steeper by being undisciplined off the field. When you aren't getting enough sleep, your performance will suffer. When you are dehydrated, your performance will suffer. When you drink alcohol, your performance will suffer. Now I'm pretty sure that you already know all that; so what's the point in telling you something you already know? Well, despite your best intentions, your need for belonging can quickly lead to some seriously self-destructive behaviors.

It's important to remember that those twenty-three helium balloons are not clones of one another. Each one of them is going to be impacted differently, even when existing in the exact same environment. It doesn't matter if all twenty-three of you decide to stay up all night partying; the effects will be more damaging to some than to others.

I may have had a bit too much to drink after passing my one-mile run. I had survived something that many of my peers had not, and I was delighted. So were my surviving teammates. So naturally we celebrated.

The next morning at soccer practice, many of my teammates seemed perfectly fine. Me? Notsomuch. I was genuinely astonished by the devastating impact of my consumption. *What was I thinking?* It was a tremendous struggle to just go unnoticed, which quickly became my primary objective for that session. College workouts are meant to separate players based on ability, fitness and grit, and I had handicapped myself with a completely avoidable, self-inflicted wound.

My point is this: Just because everyone does it, it doesn't mean that you'll all fall equally. And since you don't know exactly how far you'll fall, and since it's in your best interest not to fall at all, I highly recommend that you avoid engaging in any behaviors that will be less than conducive to your very best performance. I made it through that miserable day, but I knew that was a mistake I wouldn't make twice. I vowed to be a better, more committed athlete, and I spent the next four years backing up that promise.

Remember the story about Richard Hatch from *Survivor*? Well, this is another reason why it's so important to have a plan in place before fall ball begins. This is why it's a great idea to have a contract with yourself. You need to make a commitment to focusing all of your energies into delivering your best possible performance, and a major part of that is going to mean saying no to some social opportunities.

The social life is going to sink some of your teammates, in fall ball and beyond. Believe me, it will. If the person you are targeting wants to self-destruct, just stay out of her way. Let her create the separation for you. All you have to do is maintain your pace while she falls behind.

You have four years of college life. Don't try to cram it all in to the first ten days! As a matter of fact, you should commit to keeping those social opportunities out of your life for the first two weeks of your first semester on campus. Two weeks later you won't regret missing that party; but if you're sitting on the bench, you may very well regret attending it.

Not everything is under your control, but some things are. When you have the opportunity to control something that affects your performance, you've got to own it! Remember why you came to that college in the first place. Be strong enough to sidestep temptation so you can make your best possible case. If you don't, you will most certainly regret it.

33

THE THREE QUEENS

Let me introduce you to your three best friends for surviving your first semester of college softball: Sleep, Water, and Ice.

SLEEP - Unless you join the military, the fall of your first year is going to be the most physically grueling experience of your life. You'll be married to 6 a.m. lifts and a host of challenging new physical adventures that will push your body in ways you've never imagined. You're going to be tired –every day. You're going to be in pain –every day. And you're going to have to push through it and keep playing –every day!

You can't avoid the pain and the fatigue, but you can manage it. The better you manage it, the better you'll perform.

Sleep whenever you can for as long as you can. When you have lift at 6 a.m., class until 2 p.m. and practice at 6 p.m., nap time from 2-3 p.m. is your new best friend. An extra hour of sleep can make a world of difference. Sleeping won't be the hard part; the hard part will be just getting to your bed. If you don't prioritize sleep, you'll find reasons to cheat yourself out of it.

When you finish lunch, instead of sitting at the table and socializing for an hour, socialize for fifteen minutes and then make a bee-line for your bed. Take advantage of opportunities to sleep whenever possible. You want to stay as fresh as possible to maintain your highest level of performance.

WATER - Water is the closest thing your body has to a magic potion. Proper hydration is extremely important, particularly in the heat of September. It will speed your recovery; it will help your performance; and it will help prevent injuries and heat exhaustion. And as we discussed in the last chapter, fall ball is often a matter of attrition. If you're not hydrated, you'll never stay in the race.

ICE - By now you've probably experienced a situation where a little knock that you took during a game is suddenly much more painful a day later. That's not some type of enigma. That's just how your body works. During the fall, you're going to be taking some knocks, some bigger than others, and if you don't treat them, they'll all hurt a lot more the next day.

If you've taken some lumps —even some small ones —get ice on them immediately after your session. You should spend a good bit of your fall wrapped in ice. While water helps your body recover from the inside, ice is helping it recover from the outside.

If you have access to a cold pool, spend twenty minutes in it. And make sure you ice that arm! If this sounds like torture to you, I really don't care. I'm not saying you'll enjoy it; I'm saying it'll be worth it.

Even if you maximize your opportunities to sleep, drink water and ice yourself, you still may be in some pain. You'll just have to trust me that the pain you experience will be significantly less than if you hadn't done those things.

These are three things that are within your control. Don't be too lazy to pay attention to them.

Let me give you one other bonus tip that can be incredibly useful. If you are particularly stiff, sore or tight before a workout, pedal a stationary bike for 5-10 low-impact minutes to loosen up your legs. It'll do you a world of good.

34

RITES
OF PASSAGE

As a college rookie, you may feel like a mule, particularly during the fall. You'll be asked to do more than your fair share of picking up equipment and bagging balls and moving tees. Why? Because you're a rookie, and being a mule is just a rite of passage that all rookies must endure. Every player before you has gone through it and a year later, you'll enjoy watching the new class of rookies doing the lion's share of the grunt work. So, don't wait to be asked, volunteer! It's called servant leadership. Do it from the very first practice and don't stop doing it. Even if captains and returning players take the lead, jump right in there. Be seen doing the grunt work. Your teammates will notice. So will your coaches.

A surefire way to end up ostracized from your team is to skate these duties. It may seem silly or stupid to you, but to the players ahead of you, it is not. They served their time and they expect you to also serve yours. And your fellow rookies, well, they won't appreciate your disappearing act when it's time to do a little dirty work. Trust me, you're way better off just serving with a smile on your face than by butting heads with the system.

And since you have to endure these rites of passage anyway, you may as well use them to your advantage. Instead of just tolerating them, attack them! Do them with enthusiasm! Don't just pick up the balls; pick them up with gusto! Be the leader who gets the other rookies on board when it's time to do the chores. Your enthusiasm will be contagious, which will make the work more enjoyable. Plus, it will help establish you as a leader, and believe me, your coach will notice.

35

THE PENAL
SYSTEM

It doesn't matter how much the coach likes you, if you break a rule, there's going to be a consequence. There has to be. Why? Because coaches are forever concerned about setting dangerous precedents. When it comes to the standards of the team, everyone must be held accountable, and that duty ultimately falls to the coach. When coaches fail to hold players accountable, chaos quickly overruns the program.

If you stumble into a situation that involves some type of punishment, do yourself a favor and just take it like a champ. Don't stand there arguing your case. Just nod your head and say thank you and get on with it. And for heaven's sake, don't drag your teammates down with you. If Susie got away with one and you didn't, then so be it. Just swallow your feelings of grave injustice and accept that life isn't always fair.

I once had a rookie, Katy, who was destined to be an All-Conference player. From the moment she first stepped on the field, that much was obvious. She was athletic, quick, tall and strong. She had a cannon for an arm, hit towering dingers, and played with this wonderfully reckless abandon. I was absolutely delighted that Katy had chosen my university. So naturally she went out one Friday night, got sideways drunk and threw up on the shoes of a Resident Assistant in her dorm.

Next thing you know, Katy's parents are being called and the Student Judicial Services Committee is convened to hear her case that Monday morning.

Yes, it was a bonehead move, but when you've dug yourself a hole, the first thing you need to do is put down your shovel. And thankfully, that's exactly what Katy did.

She called me to deliver the bad news, before I had to hear about it from the Athletic Director, and that gave us a chance to get out ahead of whatever was coming next. She accepted responsibility for the entire incident and agreed to accept whatever punishment I deemed fit. We wrote a contract that included, among other things, an agreement that if there was ever a repeat of this type of incident, Katy would be removed from the team. We both signed it, and I kept it.

Katy never had another issue. She had a phenomenal career as an all-everything player. On the day she graduated, I handed her that contract and told her how proud I was of the player and person she had become.

Almost every player will have to endure some form of punishment before her career is complete. Do your best not to take it personally. Just get it done quickly *—and with dignity —*and move on to whatever's next.

36

JUST
SAY NO

Hazing is illegal and it's almost a thing of the past, but that doesn't mean that some teams don't still engage in it. If it's going to happen, it will happen during the fall. Don't put yourself at risk just to fit in with the group. If you end up in an uncomfortable situation, have the courage to stand up for yourself and walk away.

Listen to me: Your coach doesn't want the returning players to haze the rookies because it will cost him his job. If your older teammates attempt to haze the rookies, don't be afraid to notify your coach so he can put a stop to it. I know it's a difficult thing to do, but it'll be better for everyone in the end.

You're going to experience tremendous amounts of peer pressure in college. It'll be even worse for you because you're an athlete with a degree of celebrity. That makes you a trophy of sorts. When you arrive at college, you're expected to be old enough to know the difference between right and wrong and to act accordingly. Keep that in mind. It's not just about knowing what's right and what's wrong; it's also about the *action* you take.

Don't let other people, teammates or not, talk you into doing things you're not comfortable with. Be strong enough to stand your ground! Your peers will respect your courage.

SECTION 4

PLAYING
TIME

37

THE THREE
TIERS

When it comes to playing time, there are three tiers to a college softball team:

- Starter
- Reserve
- Roster

The starters and the reserves are the players who actually get on the field on game day. The roster players are the ones who fill the roster and fight to climb the ladder.

Here's what you need to remember: There is a constant shifting amongst these tiers. Players are continually moving up or down depending on performance, injuries, illness and suspensions. If you start out as a roster player, don't make the mistake of thinking that has to be your permanent address.

Making the squad is a very reasonable goal for any rookie who has joined a strong program. It means you're in the hunt to get on the field. Remember, not everyone made the team. You did! You got your foot in the door! Don't devalue yourself by giving up the fight. Contribute all you can to making your team better while working hard to improve your own game.

It'll be pretty easy to know where you stand on that ladder after a week or two of games. If you're a starter, then obviously you're doing something right. But be aware that you do not own that spot; you are just renting it by the day. There are people on a lower tier who want what you have, so you better keep working hard to defend it.

38

THE TRUTH
ABOUT
PLAYING TIME

Playing time is the currency of athletics. Your identity and your celebrity are inextricably linked to the number of innings you spend on the field. Your coach knows that. And your coach knows the same applies to every one of your teammates.

College softball is a cannibalistic frenzy for playing time. Everyone wants to graduate to the tier above, but no one is lowering a rope to lift up the teammates on the tier below. There's a lot of emotion tied into the prospect of playing time, but none of that matters when it comes time for your coach to choose a lineup.

Before we go any further, you need to understand that regardless of how good you think you are, you are not entitled to playing time. You're not playing club softball any more. Those showcase days are gone. There are no more league rules that say you have to play at least three innings of the game. Your parents aren't paying league dues. As a matter of fact, if you're on an athletic scholarship, the softball team is paying you; that makes you an employee. You've reached a level where softball is no longer about participation; now it's about results.

Only ten players get to be in the lineup at any given time. Someone has to decide who the best ten players are, and that job falls to the coach. It is her job to evaluate talent. Why? Because somebody must.

Remember, your coach has a job she wants to keep and that all hinges on winning softball games. That means her decisions about playing time are going to be based on winning. She gives playing time to the players whom she feels give the team the best chance to win games. If she believes you'll help the team win, you'll get on the field. Period.

If you're not getting the playing time you want from college softball, the rest of this section will help you understand how to deal with your predicament and give yourself the best chance of earning more time.

39

YOU DON'T
CONTROL
PLAYING TIME

Before you bury yourself under the stress of not playing, accept that you aren't the one who controls your playing time; your coach does. I know this is much easier said than done, but you've got to stay focused on the things you can control, and you can start with your effort.

Here's my advice: Focus on doing your very best and competing your hardest and outworking everyone each and every day. Don't focus on the end (playing time); focus on the process of becoming the best player you can possibly be. As you become a better player, your chances of playing more will improve.

When you focus on your playing time, you're burdening yourself with a lot of unnecessary stress. I've seen players so consumed with why they weren't playing that they completely ruined their college softball experience and even took some teammates down in the process. Don't get tangled up in the things you can't control. It's a battle you'll never win and it will sap the life right out of you.

I don't know why you started playing softball, but I know why you stuck with it; you kept coming back to softball because it was fun. You enjoyed it so you kept playing it. Don't let playing time suck the fun out of this sport you love. You'll only hurt your own cause.

Playing time is first won on the practice field. Period. You'll play better when you focus on giving your best effort and keeping the game enjoyable. Anything else you do will be counterproductive to your cause. Control what you can control and then hope for the best.

Sitting on the bench can be the most emotionally traumatizing part of a player's college softball experience. You went to college to play college softball, not watch it. You've never been told you're not good enough. You've probably started every game for every team you've ever been a part of, and now you're relegated to the role of spectator. It can be frustrating and maddening and all of that negative emotion can burn a hole through your stomach. I totally get it. But no matter the level of your anguish, you've got to find a way to manage it that will be in the best interest of both you and your team.

40

YOUR
TEAMMATES
DON'T CONTROL
THEIR PLAYING
TIME
EITHER

If you're one of those players who is going to obsess over playing time, prepare yourself to walk down a path filled with landmines. It won't take you long to pick a starter who you feel that you are better than, and she will become the target of your scorn.

Listen to me. It is silly and dangerous to be scornful of a teammate who is playing in front of you. Why? Because you don't decide your playing time and she doesn't decide hers either. If you're upset that Jenny is playing in front of you, don't blame Jenny. She's just doing her best because she wants the same thing that you want. It's not her fault. Jenny's not the idiot who can't seem to recognize your softball genius; that idiot is your coach. But that *idiot* controls the lineup and you have not convinced him that you are the player who gives his team the best chance of winning.

When you start dragging teammates into your personal house of misery, you become a cancer to your team and it won't be long before the coach decides the team is better off without you.

If you want to ignore my advice and make playing time your problem, then at least make sure you contain it as *your* problem.

41

YOUR FRIENDS WILL LIE TO YOU

When you start campaigning to your teammates and friends about the playing time you *should* be getting, you're going to find a lot of people who agree with you. You're going to say that you don't understand why the coach can't see that you are so much better than Kelly; and your friends will say, "Oh I know! You are totally better than she is!"

And guess what... they're lying to you. Why? Mainly because they love you and they want to support you. And also, because no one wants to be the one who tells you that Kelly is actually better than you. It takes a lot of courage to look you in the eye and tell you that the coach is actually right, and not a lot of people have that much courage in their tank.

Incidentally, if you start campaigning, remember that you are putting your friends into a very awkward position. By supporting you, they are betraying another teammate, and no matter what they say to your face, they won't enjoy being cornered like that. A player who takes her playing time campaign to her teammates will quickly become a major annoyance to those teammates.

Your teammates are all fighting their own battles. You can't expect them to passionately take up your cause as well. They want to play and they want to win and they want their team to get along. That's about the extent of it. Your battle is ultimately yours to fight and fight alone.

If you find yourself in this situation, it may be worth asking yourself why everyone is on your side except the coach. Is it actually that the coach is blind? Or is there just a small chance that maybe your friends are taking your side because it's the easiest way to keep the peace?

Look, it's difficult when you're not getting the playing time you think you deserve. Believe me, I know. But regardless of how badly it hurts, you've got to manage your pain with dignity. You've got to find a way to put the team first and stay loyal to the mission. You're all grown up now. By now you should know that life isn't always fair and that it doesn't always work out the way you would like. Even in the most difficult times, you've got to find a way to rise above your personal grief and present your best self.

42

LOVE YOUR
NOSE

There's another excellent way to disqualify yourself and it has nothing to do with team rules, but it has everything to do with attitude.

Let me make this impossible to misunderstand: Don't be a brat.

Yes, you may be genuinely disenchanted with your playing time and you may feel wholly justified in projecting that disenchantment, but when the spirit moves you to project, don't. Just don't.

There is nothing more annoying than a player whose body language screams, *"Look at how unhappy I am!"* Your coach knows that you really want to play, but that's not a good enough reason for your coach to put you on the field. For you to play, you have prove that you'll actually help the team win games, and you'll never do that by acting like a brat.

When the game ends, your attitude should reflect the team's success, not your own. If your team wins a game, the last thing in the world your coach wants to see is a player pouting because she didn't get to play. Yeah, it may be hard for you to control your emotions, but sometimes you just have to be a good actor. Sometimes you just have to put on a brave face and save your tears until you get into your car to drive home.

Of course there are other ways to pout, and you won't be the one to invent any of them. Disgruntled players will use all types of bad body language to express their discontent; they'll start mailing in their effort at training; they'll give the coach the silent treatment. Believe me, your coach has seen it all and has gotten over it. Incidentally, few things will come off quite so foolish as complaining about your playing time when your team has just won five games in a row.

Look, when you project your personal misery onto the team, you're going to aggravate your coach and hurt your own cause. No coach is going to reward a player for acting like a brat. No one in his right mind wants to set that type of precedent! I've dealt with four decades worth of disgruntled players; do you honestly think I'm going to cave because you gave me your pouty face? Your coach is trying to protect his job and his paycheck and if that comes at the cost of your unhappiness, then so be it. This isn't rec softball.

Somewhere along the line someone may have convinced you that the squeaky wheel gets the grease. Well, when it comes to college softball, the squeaky wheel gets replaced. Coaches get paid to coach and win, not to babysit. It doesn't take a coach very long to decide that his team and his life would both be better off without a disgruntled player.

When you put your personal unhappiness ahead of the team, you'll just end up cutting off your nose to spite your face. Your coach holds the ultimate trump card and there is not a thing in the world you can do about that. You need to find a better way to make your case.

43

POSITIONING
AND THE
GREAT MISTAKE

There are two ways to be a starter:

- Be the best player in that position
- Be the second best player when the best player becomes unavailable

If you are not a starter, it's because you aren't one of the best ten players —at least not yet. This is not a time to panic and it's not a time to give up the fight. It's a time to give yourself the best possible chance to get on the field. In short, it's time to become the best of the rest.

I'm going to share with you a story that repeats itself each year at universities throughout the country.

After the fall play day or first scrimmage with an outside opponent, a loose hierarchy will have developed and players will have a fairly good idea of the tier that they inhabit. The problem is that some players forget that this hierarchy is not iron clad. They get so deflated after two games that they give up hope on the rest of the year. Immediately there's a noticeable decline in their training habits and their intensity level and they look nothing like the player who arrived full of excitement and determination. At team meetings, their minds are somewhere other than in the room. Everything they do says, "I'm just going through the motions." In short, they check out. And checking out is the great mistake. All sorts of things can happen to bump your level between October and the start of your competitive season in February.

You have to understand that a lot can and will happen. The players who started the first game will not start every game, and there are a variety of reasons why. Some of those players will get injured or ill. Some will get suspended. Some will slump. Some will just get outplayed. These things happen all the time. The tier you inhabit doesn't have to be your permanent address. But if you're going to advance up the ladder, it won't happen by accident.

Instead of checking out, let's go the opposite direction and start thinking about *positioning*. Let's say you're an outfielder, but you're not one of the three starting outfielders. The starters are numbers one, two and three. Those are their positions and will stay their positions until further notice. You and the other reserve outfielders are occupying spots four, five and six. At that point, your top priority shouldn't be to win the starting spot —remember you don't control playing time; your top priority should be securing yourself in the number four spot. Should any of those three spots become available, you want to be next in line. Now, you don't want the starters to get injured or to fail, but if something like that happens, you most certainly want to be the one who picks up the crumbs.

When you're not the #1, you've got to put your faith in the long haul. You've got to keep bringing your very best on a daily basis and hoping that your hard work will eventually get rewarded. You can't give up the fight after a day or a week or a month. If you want to eventually become a starter, then you have to train like one on a daily basis. It might not reap rewards as quickly as you like, but then again, it might. Either way, the coach is going to notice. The coach knows who his starters are, but he is always making calculations about who will replace them if circumstances arise.

Some of your teammates are going to check out. That's fine. It helps your cause. Just don't go down that road with them. Keep fighting for every inch, every step of the way, even when it feels like your effort is being wasted. When opportunity knocks, make sure it's you who gets to open the door.

44

TAKE THE
ANSWERS

When I first read Dan Blank's version of ROOKIE, the one written to soccer players, there was one story that really hit home for me. I mean all the lessons were relevant and could be adapted to softball, but the story about this one soccer player, well, I just found it really inspiring. And it was right here, right in this chapter. So instead of trying to replace it, I'm going to sit this chapter out and allow my co-author to step up and share this story, exactly as it appeared in the soccer version of ROOKIE. But don't tune out just because it's not a softball story. The story might not be for softball, but the lesson most definitely is. So read it, enjoy it and digest it. I'll see you in the next chapter.

Here's the thing about your coach… He's sort of like a professor who has decided to feed you the answers to the next exam. That's literally what he attempts to do. Every day your coach tries to feed you the answers to a one-question exam, and the question is: *How do I get on the field?*

When you're trying to position yourself as the best of the rest, you've got to be smart enough to take those answers. It was actually a player who made me realize this.

In my current job, I am in charge of coaching the defenders at the University of Georgia. Every Tuesday night I meet with the defenders to review video of our most recent games. At certain points I'll freeze the video and ask the players, "Okay, what should happen next?" Or, "Where should this player be moving to?" I want each player to understand not only her position, but also the positions of all the other defenders. So I show them these situations and ask them to give me the answers.

A few years ago, during one of these meetings, I noticed that one player was answering the majority of the questions, and she wasn't exactly knocking people out of the way to do it. She would sit there and wait until it was obvious that no one else knew the answer, and then she would, almost regretfully, answer the question with absolute precision.

That's not the amazing part; the amazing part is that this player, Jenna Buckley, wasn't one of the starters. The starters could answer most of the questions, but not all of them. Jenna, on the other hand, could spit out the answer to each and every question I asked. This became a bit of a trend. Week after week we would get to a question that had everyone stumped, and I could tell the other players in the room were just waiting for Jenna to chime in and bail them out.

After one of these meetings, when her teammates were out of earshot, I quietly asked Jenna how she always knew the answers. She shrugged and said, "I just pay attention."

What a revolutionary concept!

I give my defenders a handbook that details our system and how to play it. I watch video with them at least once a week. And oh yeah, I work with them on the field. The questions I ask during videos aren't brain-busters; they are things we've covered time and time again. Every day I gave them the answers, but only one player was really paying close attention.

Jenna could have easily checked out. She wasn't starting and we almost never substitute our defenders. Jenna was a very talented player, but her chances of playing were slimmer based solely on her position. Still, she paid attention. And yes, she took the answers.

A few weeks later our starting center back got injured very late in a game. Jenna got to start the next game and she was absolutely sensational! Her understanding of the position was so remarkable that by the end of the game, Jenna Buckley was anointed as our new starting center back. Three months later, her teammates elected her as captain.

Jenna never checked out. Her training habits never dipped. She focused on the things she could control and did her best to own every single one of those things. And she paid attention. When I fed her the answers, she was clever enough to process and internalize them.

I don't care what sport you play, your coach wants to see you do well. He wants you to succeed. That's why he gives you the answers day after day after day. That's not by accident. If you want to ace the test, you've got to be smart enough to take advantage of his generosity.

And oh by the way, I hope you realize that we've been feeding you answers since you started reading this book. That's not by accident either. The question is: *Have you been paying attention?*

45

YOUR MOST
ABUNDANT
AND UNDERVALUED
RESOURCE

You're going to have a lot of teammates, and none of them are clones. They all bring something decidedly unique to the table. They all have something that got them to the college level. And you can learn something from each one of them.

I've had the opportunity to watch fantastic youth players arrive to the college level and stagnate almost immediately. But I've also watched role players evolve into college stars due to a steady improvement in their individual games. It's remarkable how many of the players in the latter group began to resemble their more high-profile teammates in terms of their technical skill sets. Their strength improved as did their throwing ability, hitting and bunting ability. In a sense, they began to mirror the skill sets of the players who played the most innings. Why? Because they saw something they liked from a teammate and decided to make it a part of their own games. Makes a lot of sense, right?

Someone on your team is going to be an awesome bunter. She never whiffs and the ball always dies close to the foul line. Most of your teammates will say, *"Wow, So and so sure is great at bunting! I don't know how she does it!"* You, on the other hand, can take a radically different approach and simply ask her to teach you how she does it. If you can master that skill, you've just added one more tool to your toolbox and become a better player in the process.

To improve at a noticeable level, you have to do more than just show up. Yes, you will naturally improve simply by playing every day and adjusting to the new level of play, but that's a slow climb. Wouldn't you prefer to accelerate the process? Of course you would! And you can! You just need to study the best things that your teammates have to offer and then learn to do those things as well as they do.

Your teammates will give you a buffet of choices for technical improvements. You don't need to reinvent the wheel; just take the best parts of everybody else's wheels! You'll begin to do this anyway without even realizing it. The key is to do it *while* realizing it! The key is to enter college softball with the premeditated idea of borrowing the best that your teammates have to offer and incorporating those things into your own game. The more tools you can add to your toolbox, the better player you will be. And remember, the best players play.

Coaches aren't the only learning aids at your disposal. Pay attention to your teammates. Take their best ideas and add them to your game.

And, just as an FYI, this borrowing of ideas isn't limited to players. Coaches constantly take the best things they can from other coaches to make their own team better. There are only a few things our club did that were truly our own.

46

CHARITY
TIME

Despite what I've led you to believe, there are actually moments when playing time doesn't go to the very best player. Sometimes, when the score is out of reach and the result has been decided, the coach will have the luxury of giving other players their chance. Let's refer to these moments as charity time. And believe me, you want a piece of them! But before you have a chance to take advantage of charity time, the coach still has to pick you.

When your coach is deciding who gets the charity time, she's either going to choose the players she wants to see... or the players she wants to *reward*. If there's a tie between two players in terms of talent, the coach is going to pick the player she likes best. She's going to pick the player who has earned the reward by doing the right things, consistently working hard, presenting a positive attitude and being a good, responsible teammate. This might be the time when picking up all that equipment comes back to bless you.

Everything we've been discussing for the past several chapters has been about positioning yourself. Charity time is where all that positioning can pay off.

Understand that charity time will typically come in small portions, usually 1-3 innings or a pinch-hit spot. Doesn't matter. Don't feel as if you're above playing the final inning of an 8-0 game. Do not underestimate the value of charity time. Any amount of time is more than nothing and it gives you a chance to make a statement, no matter how brief. If you can string together enough of those small statements, you begin to make a real case for yourself.

I've seen too many rookies stuck on the bench because they weren't ready to play when their number was called, mainly because they had the pouty face all week because life wasn't giving them exactly what they wanted, exactly when they wanted it, and instead of grinding to improve, they focused their energies on showing the world exactly how disenchanted they were with the great injustice that had befallen them. They made the great mistake of checking out, so when they finally got the chance to take center stage, they were unprepared physically, mentally and emotionally. Charity time only matters if you can take advantage of it.

Now understand, very rarely does a player go from not playing at all to starting in one swing of the bat. A starting position is usually won in chunks —one small chunk at a time. When charity time comes your way, make the most of it. For starters, don't take the field to maintain the status quo. Regardless of whether you are winning or losing, take the field with the goal of *changing the game*. If that game is a dying body, make it your mission to be the AED that shocks it back to life!

When you're handed charity time, you've got nothing to lose! What's the worst that can happen? You're already not playing! Use your handful of innings or your one at-bat to showcase the turbo-charged force I know you to be! Believe me, if you buzz around that field like a runaway band saw, your coach is going to notice and she's going to like it and her trust in you will grow.

Charity time can be your chance to turn one inning today into seven innings next week. Don't scoff at the opportunity. Take advantage of it!

47

BASS PLAYER
WANTED

Getting on the field is good; staying on the field is better! Let's talk about one excellent strategy for maximizing your innings.

Do you know who Adam Clayton is? No? Well, I'm sure you've heard his music. He's the bass player for U2. You're probably more familiar with his bandmate, Bono.

Every band has its front person. He's the lead singer. His face is on the album covers. He's the one doing all the media interviews. He's the one the fans really want to see when they pay money to go to a concert. Bono is U2's front man, and since the late 1970s, the band has been selling millions of records and making millions and millions of dollars. U2 has cemented its reputation as one of the greatest rock and roll bands of all time. And yet you've never heard of Adam Clayton. Strange, right?

Softball teams operate with a similar dynamic. Each team has one or two or three stars. These are the players who hit dingers or throw no hitters. These are the players that pay your coach's mortgage, so he gives them a little more freedom to freelance when the game is underway. He may give them a permanent green light to steal, or let them swing away on a 3-0 count, and do some other things that he doesn't accept from the other players on the team. It's important to note that they were given these freedoms because they've proven themselves as stars; they didn't become stars because they were given these freedoms. Remember that.

To be good at your job, you have to know how you fit into the team. If you're a star, trust me, you'll know. If you're not (and 99% of us are not), it's okay. You can still be a great player and a vital part of the team's success without being in the spotlight. But you have to make peace with who you are and what your role is within your team. When you confuse who you are with what is expected of you, you're going to have problems.

Generally speaking, we ask our stars to win games for us. We ask that our non-stars —our mortals —keep us in the game. We want them to be reliable. We want them to field, throw, get a base hit or put down a decent bunt. We want them to do the grunt work. We want them to do their job well enough that we have a chance to win the game.

If you're having trouble following me, watch some college or professional basketball games. The star is the person who has the ball in their hands when the team is down by a point and there are three seconds left on the clock. The reason this player has the ball is because they are the person who is most likely to win the game for the team and the coaches and teammates know that. So, they give this player the ball and get out of their way and let them do what they do best.

Imagine if by some miracle you ended up playing for the Los Angeles Lakers and your team was down a point and there were ten seconds left and you had the ball in your hands. At the top of the key stands LeBron James with his hands out, begging for you to pass him the ball. But instead of passing to LeBron, you drive to the basket, lean in for the lay-up, and your shot gets swatted down to the other end of the floor. Now, doesn't that seem idiotic? Of course it does! Why? Because LeBron is already surrounded by players who are much better than you —legitimate superstars… multi-millionaires —and even they know to get him the ball when the game is on the line.

Who you are right now is who you are. You have physical and technical limitations. Over time you will improve on those areas and maybe one day you'll become the star, but for now, who you are is who you are. And who you are today should dictate your role within the team.

Since you're not a star just yet, don't worry about playing like one. Right now your objective is to get and stay on the field. You do that by earning the trust of your coach. You earn this trust by playing your role, by executing your duties, and by *being responsible.* I cannot overstate how important that last one is. You'll never stay on the field if you consistently throw the ball away, strike out looking, or make base-running errors. You need to show the coach that you're playing for his team, not the opponents.

As you are fighting to make a case for yourself, let me give you some advice: Do the simple things consistently well. Make the out on defense, catch the can-of-corn pop up, lay down the sac bunt, hustle on the basepaths. Don't worry too much about impacting the score-line just yet; you'll have plenty of chances to do that when you're an established presence. For now, just worry about proving that you can be trusted. Keep it simple. Execute the simple things on a consistent basis and your stock will rise.

That doesn't sound very glamorous, does it? No, it surely doesn't. But until you are a fixture in the lineup, you need to build your case one safe play at a time. You won't ever be a star if you can't stay on the field. Right now just focus on doing your part to help the team win games.

What I'm trying to say is this: Don't be afraid to be the bass player. Not everyone gets to be the lead singer. Adam Clayton's net worth is roughly $150 million. Why? Because when the band sells records, the bass player gets paid too.

48

FEEDBACK

If you're not playing as much as you like, I assure you it's not because the coach doesn't want her best players on the field. So the question that you need to ask isn't: *Why am I not playing?* The question you need to ask is: *What can I do to become a better player?* And the person you want to answer that question is your coach.

Periodically asking for feedback is a good idea, even if you're a fixture in the starting lineup. None of us are beyond improvement. And if you're not reaching your playing-time goals, then you have an even clearer reason for soliciting your coach's opinions. Your coach will be happy to offer you suggestions because your personal improvement is in the team's best interest.

When it comes to soliciting feedback, there are some things to keep in mind. First of all, you probably get feedback every day when you're on the practice field. Make sure you're improving on the things that have already been asked of you.

Secondly, there's a fine line between asking for feedback and campaigning for playing time. When you ask a coach why you aren't starting or why you aren't playing more, it doesn't matter what words actually come out of her mouth, the answer can be translated to: *Right now, there are some players who are better than you.*

Instead of asking why you're not playing, try phrasing your query like this: *Coach, I'd like to try to earn more playing time. What areas do you think I should be focusing on to improve?*

Now, when your coach takes the time to answer that question, she isn't talking just to hear herself speak. Some players constantly ask for feedback as a way to feign interest in actually improving. If you're going to ask your coach for feedback, follow through by putting in the time and effort to improve, and that probably means coming out to practice early or staying late.

Let me clear up another wonderful misconception about putting in the extra time. Some players feel that if they set up an extra training session or two with the coaches that they'll automatically receive more playing time as a reward for putting in a few extra hours of work. That's not how it works. This isn't like turning in an extra-credit assignment to bring up your grade in history class. You don't train more to get more playing time. *You train more to become a better player.* When you become a better player, then your chances of playing more will naturally improve. Ultimately your playing time isn't determined by the amount of hours you log; it's determined by your ability to help the team win.

When your coach gives you feedback, she has done you a tremendous favor because again, she has fed you the answers. You have to be smart enough to capitalize on her generosity by putting in the right kind of work to become a better player.

49

CHANGE
THE WAY
YOU PLAY

At our end-of-season individual meetings, we inevitably have this conversation with one of our first-years. When she was playing for her club, she was much more dominant than she was as a college rookie. That's only natural. At the club level she competed against players her own age and there were geographic restrictions on the available talent pools. When she gets to college, she is playing against players who are three years older and who come from all over the country. Even some of her fellow first-years are just plain better than she is. The speed of play is faster, the skill level is better, the pitching is better and the players are smarter tactically. She *shouldn't* be as dominant as she was in the club system. The things she got away with down there won't always work so well up here. But the biggest problem she faced came from her own brain because she refused to adapt to the demands of her new environment.

The jump from club/high school softball to college softball is immense. College softball is club ball on steroids. College softball is a club softball all-star game, and some of those all-stars have the benefit of two or three years of experience under their belts. You can't expect to waltz in and have everything work as well as it did when you were in high school. You should enter college softball with the understanding that you're going to have to change some things about the way you play. You have to adapt to survive. It's softball's brand of Darwinism.

You have strengths and you have weaknesses, and some things that were legitimate strengths in high school are now just average abilities in your new world. Speed is an easy example. Many who were the fastest player on their high school teams wouldn't finish amongst the top ten in a race against their college teammates. Remember –bigger pond, bigger fish.

You may have been a dominant pitcher in high school or club, but guess what… you're now trying to pitch against the cream of the crop. They're bigger, faster, stronger, smarter and as a bonus, they'll have access to scouting reports and video. They're going to be more organized. They'll have a hitting plan. Your pitching will be studied closely by every batter. You won't get away with a meatball down the middle of the plate.

These are among the most common issues that players are faced with when they get to the bigger pond. You'll figure out what works for you pretty quickly. You may have been the fastest player on your high school team and then find that you are also the fastest player on your college team as well. If you are, well then rock on! But chances are, when you get to college, some of your strengths aren't as mighty as you once thought.

Knowing your strengths is the easy part. The tricky part is letting go of the things that will no longer work for you. If you can't let go of those things, you'll just end up banging your head against a wall. Some things just won't work for you, no matter how hard you work at them. Sometimes hard work just isn't enough. Sometimes you're better off changing what you're working hard at.

You need to identify your new weaknesses. Accept your limitations and create a plan to reinvent yourself. Your ability to adapt will determine whether you stagnate or keep improving. If you stagnate, you'll see a flood of teammates passing you by in the quest for playing time.

At the end of your first season of college softball, you should be able to definitively answer this question: *How have I changed as a player?* You should be able to produce some type of clear cut answer. In some form or fashion, there should be something different about the way you think and play the game. If there isn't, you are failing to adapt.

I guarantee you that your coaches will have given you plenty of feedback on how they want you to change as a player, even if you haven't asked for it. It's up to you to process that feedback and use it to your advantage to become a better college softball player.

50

THE RESPONSE

As we discussed, the tiers on a team are fluid. Players move up and down the ladder. Mostly we've been discussing how to get to the highest tier. But what happens when you reach that top tier and then get bumped down? This can be the most frustrating and emotionally charged experience of your college softball career. Handling it with dignity is much easier said than done, so let's prepare your response before you're caught by surprise.

Telling a regular that she won't be in tomorrow's starting lineup is one of the most difficult things a coach has to do. But when he does it, you can bet that he's looking for a certain type of reaction from the player who was just relegated to the bench. Believe me when I tell you that the proper reaction to this adversity can go a long, long way in getting you back on the field sooner rather than later.

Earlier we mentioned that there are times when you're just going to have to be a good actor, and this may be one of them. When the coach gives you that news, swallow the lump in your throat, look the coach in the eye, and in the sincerest voice you can muster, say, "Ok Coach, whatever you think is best for the team." That's it. There doesn't need to be any more conversation and frankly, you probably don't want there to be. As soon as the coach says, "Thank you," turn and walk out of that room and find a quiet place to calm yourself.

In these situations, many players feel betrayed. I guess that's just natural because you'll inevitably feel a sense of ownership over a starting spot. You'll begin to think of it as yours and yours alone. However, as we've said from the very beginning, no one owns a starting spot; everyone is just renting, and that includes you. Moving players in and out of the starting lineup is just part of the business. And let's face it; when you were the starter, you weren't feeling sorry for the player behind you, so don't expect anyone to feel sorry for you when the winds shift. Remember, your teammates all have their own battles to fight.

When the rug gets pulled out from under you, the worst thing you can do is give up hope. Not starting this one game doesn't automatically mean that you've lost the starting spot forever. Sometimes a coach will drop a player from the lineup just to send a message, particularly if that player has been dragging at training. The hope is to light a fire under the player and hope that she responds with enough fight to win back her spot.

I've seen many cases where the replacement starter had a horrendous performance and the position defaulted straight back to the player who had been benched. The problem is that you just don't know if or when things will turn back in your favor. So what do you do? You go back to positioning. You go back to fighting for the #2 spot.

Early in my career we had a second baseman named Sara. She wasn't super flashy, and she finished her career with a whopping home run total of one. But Sara was one of the most reliable players I ever coached. Her fielding was clean, she made the plays she was expected to make, and she was a steady contact hitter who always put the ball in play. She was strictly singles and doubles, and she almost never struck out. And then one game she did. A lot. As a junior, Sara went face first into an epic slump. One game she just couldn't put the bat on the ball. No worries. We chalk it up to a bad game. Until the same thing happened the next game. And the game after that. And the game after that.

Slumps are a cyclical horror. What starts as a physical snafu will quickly morph into a psychological one. When a slump burrows into a player's psyche, that's when the real problems begin. And the worse it gets, the worse it gets. And for Sara, things had gotten really, really bad.

We ultimately reached the point where I had to tell Sara that I was sitting her down. It was a difficult conversation. Sara had owned the second base spot for two and a half seasons. Now she was being told she would have to step aside and give a freshman named Maria a chance.

I could tell that, just for a split-second, Sara thought about arguing her case, but she thought better of it. She was one of the smartest players I ever coached, and certainly smart enough to understand the reality of the situation: She was giving us absolutely nothing on offense.

When you bench someone who has been a fixture in the lineup, it's difficult to predict how that player will react. Beyond being our steadiest player, Sara was also one of our most positive, most vocal players. She was always encouraging her teammates, always rooting them on at the plate, or picking them up after an error or a strike out. But that was when she was a starter. It's easy to be supportive when you're playing every inning of every game. I was wondering how Sara-the-reserve would respond.

I really should have known better than to even ask that question. Sara was genetically programmed to be a great teammate. Of course she remained loud and positive and cheered on all of her teammates, including Maria. But she did more than just cheer.

So, Maria gets her first start and steps to the plate in the first inning and promptly whiffs on four pitches. Before she comes back to the plate to lead off the fourth, Sara pulls her aside and offers some advice.

I told you that Sara was smart. What I didn't tell you was that Sara had a wonderful knack for picking up tells from a pitcher. She watched opposing pitchers carefully, looking for little tics in their body language that might give away the next pitch. And wouldn't you know, this pitcher had a tic. By the end of the third inning, Sara suspected that when this pitcher was gearing up to throw a rise-ball, she would bring her glove all the way against her chest. But if she was going to throw a change-up, her glove would be angled slightly toward the batter.

Sara wasn't one hundred percent, proof positive, but she felt confident enough to share this little nugget with Maria before her second at-bat. The first pitch was a rise-ball out of the zone. She followed up with another rise-ball for a strike, leveling the count at 1-1. Before the third pitch, Maria noticed the pitcher's glove angled ever so slightly toward home plate, then drilled a change-up into the gap in left-center for a lead-off double. She stood on second base smiling from ear to ear, then pointed to Sara as a thank you. Sara immediately shared her intel with the rest of her teammates, we broke the game open and went on to win comfortably.

It's easy to be positive when things are going your way, but the measure of any person is found in how he or she responds to adversity. Despite the injustice that many perceived, Sara remained loyal to her teammates, coaches and the mission. Sara's display not only showcased her as a teammate we would all want, but it also positioned her as a player that her coaches wouldn't mind putting back on the field.

Sara's time on the bench didn't last long. She broke out of her slump the next game with a pinch-hit dinger (yes, her *one* home run), and morphed back into her reliable self. Sara's softball life returned to the way she wanted it, but we can learn a lot from Sara's day on the bench. You see, when you're faced with challenging situations, all that's left to do is choose how you will respond to them. Sara's response was both courageous and remarkable and it showcased her very best self.

If you are ever faced with this same predicament, I recommend you do the same.

In the meantime, let me suggest that you become your replacement's most vocal supporter. You show everyone in that dugout that you're prioritizing the team's success over your own playing time. Chances are that the teammate who replaced you has spent many games cheering her butt off for you. Now it's time for you to return the favor.

Anything less than this reaction… anything less than full-throated support of your teammates and one-hundred percent effort in practice will only hurt your own cause. I'm not saying it's easy to swallow your pride and put on a brave face. I'm just saying that it's the best possible response that gives you the most expedient path to winning back your position. Plus, years down the road, you'll look back and realize that quite simply, it was the right thing to do.

SECTION 5

TEAM
CULTURE

51

IT'S CHEMICAL

Team chemistry is impossible to measure and also impossible to miss. It is a vital part of any successful college softball program. It's very difficult to battle your opponents when you're constantly stopping to battle yourself. Good chemistry can take a team to unbelievable heights, while bad chemistry can dismantle the most talented team.

Team chemistry is an undeniable factor in the success of any program, and it's everyone's job to protect it. Even you, Rookie.

You'll hear this many more times before your career is finished, but once you join that college softball team, your actions affect far more than just you. Try to remember that when you're toying with the idea of doing something incredibly stupid. When your recklessness negatively affects the team, you become a chemistry problem.

52

CAT AND MOUSE

When you play club or high school softball, there tends to be a cat and mouse arrangement with the rules. The coach is the cat and the players are all mice and the rules only matter if the coach catches you breaking them. That won't be the case when you join a college program that takes itself seriously. In a college program with a strong culture, everyone is responsible for guarding the cheese.

You aren't stepping into a team; you're stepping into a culture. In this culture, the rules matter. They matter to your coaches and yes, they even matter to your teammates. Chances are, your teammates had a hand in setting up the rules and the standards that govern this culture and they are proud of them.

You see, you're just a rookie and college looks like a place of infinite possibilities where you can cut loose and run wide open. But remember those seniors we talked about way back when? This is their last chance to do something fantastic as softball players. This is their last chance to shine up their legacies, and that is very important to them. And they understand the value of the rules. They understand that the rules and standards exist for a reason and that the team is better when everyone is living up to those standards, including the academic ones. And they sure as heck don't appreciate a stupid rookie screwing around with their last season of college softball. When you break the rules of your college softball program, it won't be just the coach who comes gunning for you. Your willingness to submit to the culture will have a bigger effect on your team's chemistry than you probably imagine.

Whatever culture exists around your program, your first semester is not the time to challenge it. Your rookie season is your time to embrace this new culture and simply accept it until you eventually grow to understand it. All of the silly things you don't understand exist for a reason and eventually those reasons will unveil themselves to you. And when they do, and you come to appreciate them, you'll find yourself defending them and imparting them onto a new class of rookies. Until that day arrives, put your faith in your program and trust that there are very good reasons for the things you don't yet understand.

53

NO BACKSTABBING

If you want your teammates to ostracize you in a hurry, here's a foolproof recipe: Talk badly about them behind their backs.

To be honest, I'm not really sure if it's such a good idea to even include this chapter because if you're not a person who backstabs your teammates, you don't need to read it. And if you are that type of person, I doubt that reading this book is going to save you. But I'm going to include it anyway, if for no other reason than maybe it will give you the courage to confront a teammate who begins to backstab other teammates.

Team chemistry hinges on the ability of teammates to trust one another. That will never happen when players are worried about what's being said when they aren't in the room. Incidentally, just so we are crystal clear about this, when you speak badly about a teammate behind her back, she absolutely will find out about it. Believe it! And when she does, then you've got some real problems. And chances are your team does too.

To have great teammates, you've first got to be a great teammate. For teammates to protect you, you have to be willing to protect them. Instead of slamming your teammates when they aren't around, make it your goal to protect them instead. Don't tolerate it when others start badmouthing your teammates. Don't be afraid to stand up and say, "Hey, so and so is a teammate of ours and I don't appreciate you talking behind her back like this."

Yeah, it's difficult to have the courage to stand up to anyone in a situation like this, particularly a teammate, but if you do, word will get around that you're a stand-up teammate and your street credit will go through the roof.

54

BAGGAGE

Softball practice is certainly not the place to drag your personal baggage. You and all of your teammates have plenty of battles to fight off the softball field. You've all got to deal with academic challenges and relationship issues and car troubles and money issues and the many other landmines that make up the college experience. The softball field should be a sanctuary from all of that baggage for you *and* your teammates. Softball practice should be the favorite part of your day. It should be therapeutic. You should be happy when it starts and a little bit sad when it's over. When you drag your baggage onto the field, you ruin the experience for you and also for your teammates.

You need to develop an on-off switch for your softball life. You need to compartmentalize softball as the part of your day that remains immune to all of the other stresses that might happen to consume you on any given day. If you don't, you're going to cheat yourself out of a big part of the college softball experience and you're going to negatively impact the entire culture.

You're not going to play softball forever. Chances are these are the last four meaningful years of softball that you will ever experience. Protect them! Don't waste a single day of them by allowing personal issues to contaminate your softball. It's just not worth it.

When it's time for softball, leave your baggage at the door.

55

EXIT
STRATEGY

As important as it is to leave your baggage off the softball field, it's equally important to leave your softball on the softball field.

As a college softball player, you compete against your best friends and your roommates every day. Some days you'll beat them and some days they'll beat you and sometimes it'll probably get a little bit heated and when practice ends, your pot will still be boiling. You know what? That's fabulous! That's what softball should be! What makes softball worthwhile and memorable is all the emotion that it brings out of you. Imagine if softball didn't do that. Imagine if it never made your heart race or it never made you jump in celebration or cry in defeat. If it never did any of those things, would you still love it so much? Of course not! It would be about as satisfying as cooking a reasonably good omelet.

In a strong softball culture, the players compete, and they compete to the utmost of their abilities day in and day out and they battle their teammates with the same conviction as they would battle their opponents. That's how it's supposed to work. And when it does, sometimes nerves will get a little bit frayed.

When softball is over, it's over. Don't take your individual battles back to your car or back to your dorm room. Again, you've got to compartmentalize softball to keep it from dripping into your non-softball world.

You want my advice? At the end of practice, if there's a teammate who really pushed your buttons, go shake her hand. Look her in the eye, shake her hand and tell her, *"Great job!"* It might seem strange to you and it will probably seem even stranger to her, but as soon as you do that, you're going to feel all of that anger drain right out of your body and you'll be able to move on with the rest of your day as the happy, socially well-adjusted person I know you to be.

When you take softball home with you, it's a catalyst to backstabbing, and we've already discussed what a disaster that can be. That's why it's so important that you leave your softball where it belongs —on the softball field.

56

THE BIG
NO-NO

Your teammates are going to have boyfriends or girlfriends and some of those significant others are going to be significantly good-looking. I'm sure you know where I'm heading with this and believe me, this is a line that you don't want to cross.

I don't care how good-looking that person is and I don't care how much your heart yearns for him or her, stay the heck away! Show me a college team in turmoil and I'll show you a love triangle because one teammate couldn't stay away from another teammate's boyfriend/girlfriend.

When one of these situations arises, it fractures the team because the other players are backed into taking sides. When the lines are drawn and sides are chosen, you've got feuding, in-fighting and a chemical disaster, and the healing can literally take years. You'll lose friends and gain enemies and a day or two later you'll realize what an enormous mistake you've made and how you'd give up a limb to turn back the clock and make a better decision. This is one of those topics where you can believe me now or believe me later, but eventually you will believe me.

Very few of life's issues are as clear cut, black and white as this one. When I say that your teammate's significant others are off limits, I mean 100%, no questions asked, OFF LIMITS!

57

BEING A

TEAMMATE

Being a teammate can be boiled down to one very simple phrase, a phrase that might just be my most favorite one of all: *I've got your back.*

Understand this: The second-greatest gift of being part of a team is in knowing that your teammates have your back. The greatest gift is the opportunity to also have theirs.

Yes, there is strength in numbers, but that strength is magnified by a common bond born of the shared misery of giving oneself over to the greater good. As a team, you can have power! As a team, you are much stronger than any one person standing alone. And as a team, you can stand shoulder to shoulder to fight for that in which you believe. It is a bond like nothing else you will ever again experience, and my advice to you is to squeeze that orange for every drop of juice it has to offer.

As a Rookie, your willingness to have backs can fast-track you into the team's social fabric, because if you have their backs, they'll in turn have yours. It doesn't always require something as dramatic act of heroism; it could be as simple as speaking well of a teammate when she isn't in the room. It could be helping a teammate bag the balls when it isn't your turn. It could be giving up your window seat on an airplane. Let me give you another example that you'll most certainly have the opportunity to capitalize upon.

Your first fall is a physically and emotionally grueling time, and because it is, you and your teammates will experience the deepest sleep you've ever known. And I guarantee you that if you and all your rookie classmates don't arrange to look after one another, someone is going to sleep through a training session. Believe me, it will happen. Not a good thing for the rookie or the team.

When you rise from that bed, make sure your roommates are up; then go make sure the other rookies are up. Don't leave that dorm until your entire class is accounted for. And if one of your teammates can't seem to pull herself from the covers, dump a bucket of cold water on her head. She might scream bloody murder, but she'll be thanking you for years to come.

Having backs comes in many forms and fashions. It's really just about making your teammates' lives better. It's about being unselfish and letting someone else have the first shower, or picking up the equipment when it's not your turn. It's about deflecting the praise onto your teammates when a reporter from the student newspaper asks you about your game-winning dinger. It's about showing everyone that you don't stand above the team, but that you stand with it.

To have great teammates, you must first be a great teammate. When you give yourself to the team, the team will then give itself to you.

SECTION 6

OTHER
HELPFUL HINTS

58

THE
END-OF-YEAR
MEETING

When your season ends, the coach is probably going to arrange for individual meetings with the players. This is an excellent opportunity for you to figure out exactly what you need to focus on moving into the summer and fall of your second year, and how you fit into the plans for the following season.

Give this meeting the respect it deserves. First of all, don't be late. Put a reminder in your phone or write a note on your hand; do whatever you have to do, but get there on time.

In this meeting your coach is going to ask you about your academics. He's going to ask for your thoughts on the season. He's going to ask you what you think you did well. And he is going to ask you where you think you need to improve, and your goals for making those improvements. Then he'll tell you how he would answer all those questions.

This meeting won't be horribly dramatic, but it's a good idea to have some idea of how you're going to answer those questions because it shows that you actually take the time to think about the game and evaluate your performances.

Additionally, I suggest that you bring along a pad and a pen. It will send the message that you're taking this meeting seriously, and that will impress your coach. More importantly, when the coach tells you what to work on, you won't have to worry about forgetting those things if you write them down.

A lot of players just breeze through these meetings without giving them much thought, which is unfortunate because this meeting is your springboard into your second year of college softball. Use it to clarify your training objectives so you have the best possible chance of getting or staying on the field as a sophomore. Find out exactly what the coach needs from you. Again, you will be fed the answers. And again you have to be smart enough to realize that.

Be prepared. Stay open and honest. Most importantly, take the answers.

59

THE ALUMS

There's a pretty good chance that at some point during the year you're going to encounter some type of alumni function. A bunch of people who look like they might have once been athletic are going to descend upon your program for a weekend and do whatever the heck they feel like doing. Meet your softball alumni. Once, they were the heart and soul of your college team.

One weekend a year they get to come to town and tell everyone how much harder it was back when they played and how soft the current players have gotten. Don't worry about it. Fifteen years from now you'll be doing the same thing. These alums built what you walked into. They've earned a voice. And most importantly, their presence shows that they care about the program and that they want to stay connected.

Some players dread alumni functions. Let me tell you something; those players are idiots. Those players are blind to the opportunities that these alums can provide. If a 35-year-old is coming back to your university to try to throw a softball, it's only because she is passionate about the university and your softball program. And that, Rookie, is a person that you want to know!

A well-organized alumni association is a thing of beauty. It's like the team-after-the-team. But instead of getting together to throw the ball around or trying to hit dingers, you get together to take vacations and find jobs and start businesses and plan weddings and raise money when there's been an emergency. When you graduate from college, very few of your teammates will be in much of a position to help you. They'll still be young and looking to find their own stride. They won't have many connections in the real world. Your alums on the other hand, well a lot of them are settled into great jobs and have a million connections and the one thing they desperately long to do is to help other softball players from their university. I'm not making this stuff up! Your softball alums can be some of the most powerful allies you'll ever know, but only if you actually get to know them.

You'll be a college softball player for just four years, but you'll be a softball alum for the rest of your life. When your alumni function rolls around, don't sit in a corner being afraid of the old people and looking to skip out at the first chance. They're not actually zombies. Introduce yourself with a smile and ask what the softball program was like back in the old days. They'll be happy to share their war stories with you. Those alums will latch on to you and they will remember you and they will look forward to staying in touch with you and when that happens, something good just happened to you.

Remember this: If your coach has been at the university for years, then the alumni game is one of her best days. She'll make a giant fuss over those alums because these people are family to her —just like you are, even if you don't realize it yet.

60

HORIZONS

You're going to blaze your own trail through college. You're going to make your own choices and set your own boundaries and learn from your own mistakes and in the end, all of those things both good and bad will make up the best years of your life. While you're navigating your way through this bold new world, heed this simple piece of advice: Be more than an athlete.

Outside of your classes, athletics is going to consume the lion's share of your time. You're going to spend most of your time surrounded by athletes. You'll probably live with them, eat with them and hang out with them. There's nothing inherently wrong with that. However, there's a great big other world beyond the athletes and I highly recommend that you avail yourself of this other world.

College offers you opportunities that you won't get anywhere else. You can take a kick-boxing class on Monday and host your own radio show on Tuesday and volunteer at the soup kitchen on Wednesday and star in a play on Thursday! College gives you your one real chance to dabble in a zillion different activities and to bounce around from one interest to the next with no real strings attached. College gives you the chance to socialize with people that you would never associate with outside of the bubble. Embrace this! Spend some time with the freaks and the hippies and the nerds and the artsy folks that hang out in the coffee houses. Take advantage of all of this because the moment you put on that cap and gown, the bubble bursts and the honeymoon is over and you are officially a member of the real world and your days will revolve around whichever activity pays the bills.

Take advantage of the things and the people that college offers that exist in a world beyond athletics. Don't leave college filled with regret saying, *"I wish I'd done this and I wish I'd done that."* College gives you this amazing opportunity to do this, that and a hundred other things if only you make the effort to get involved.

You have a four-year window of opportunity to fill with unbelievable life experiences. Leave college with something more than just the experience of being an athlete. You'll never regret it.

61

ACADEMICS

The day will come when college is over and you're going to want (check that... need) a job. The problem is that it can be very difficult to get an interview because you don't have any experience; but how can you ever get experience when no one will give you a job? It's the hamster wheel that college grads have been spinning since the beginning of time. But since you want to eat and pay your rent and put gas in your car, you have no choice but to keep grinding. You keep sending out resumes and knocking on doors until one day, you strike potential gold!

You find a firm that is willing to let you get your foot in the door with an interview. The leadership of this firm is pretty open-minded about giving college kids with no experience a chance to come aboard and learn as they go, but they're not willing to hire just anyone. They want an office full of the best and the brightest! They understand that you're too young to have any actual real-world experience, so they're going to judge you on the one measurable body of work you do have, and it's called your GPA. And at that moment, you'll either be thankful that you focused on your academics or regretful that you did not.

It also bears mentioning that while your GPA can get you in the room, the fact that you were a college athlete for four years can help keep you there. Employers love hiring athletes. Athletes tend to be high achievers with high work rates who do well in team settings, so what's not to love?

Trust me on this, a high GPA with collegiate athletics experience will give you a nice head start on the competition.

I hope that is all the reason you need to remember that your academics are actually important, and it starts in your freshman year.

62

FIRST-YEAR

When I went to college, first-year students were still called freshman. On move-in day, all the freshman guys were gathered in the basement lounge of our dorm to hear an address from the Dean of Students. It's funny, but I still remember that speech. Well, I remember part of it.

The Dean told us that as freshmen, that's exactly what we were: Fresh. Men. He said that what we did before we arrived at campus didn't matter anymore; that this was a chance to reinvent ourselves. Our past did not equal our future —not if we didn't want it to. Our reputations had ceased to exist. If there were things about the high school me that I didn't love, this was my shot at a reset. My past was irrelevant in my new world, mainly because nobody knew about it. I was now working with a blank slate. And Rookie, so are you.

You may be perfectly content in your own skin, and if you are, fantastic! But many of us wouldn't mind a do-over of sorts, and your first year of college is an excellent place for a do-over. Maybe you would like to be more studious, or be more social, or revamp your fashion style. Maybe you want to expand your circle of friends or get more involved in activities beyond softball. Well, I've got some good news for you… This is your time!

You are a first-year. That means this is the *first* year of your new life. You can jettison the parts of your old life that no longer serve you, and you can unveil new and improved replacement parts. And you can apply this to both your athletic and non-athletic lives.

This is your chance at a great edit. Nobody knows you, so you can't be boxed in by their expectations. This is a chance to redefine who you are in the eyes of everyone you encounter in this wonderful new existence.

This is your glorious do-over, if that's what you want it to be. This is your time now. Who do you want the world to see?

63

LOVE WHAT
YOU DO

Why We Play D3 Athletics

"It's not about getting a scholarship, getting drafted, or making Sports Center. It's a deep need in us that comes from the heart. We need to practice, to play, to lift, to hustle, to sweat. We do it all for our teammates and for the student in our calculus class that we don't even know. We don't practice with a future major league first baseman; we practice with a future sports agent. We don't lift weights with a future Olympic wrestler; we lift with a future doctor. We don't run with a future Wimbledon champion; we run with a future CEO. It's a bigger part of us than our friends and family can understand. Sometimes we play for 2,000 fans; sometimes twenty-five. But we still play hard. You cheer for us because you know us. You know more than just our names. Like all of you, we are students first. We don't sign autographs. But we do sign graduate school applications, MCAT exams, and student body petitions. When we miss a kick or strike out, we don't let down an entire state. We only let down our teammates, coaches, and fans. But the hurt is still the same. We train hard, lift, throw, run, kick, tackle, shoot, dribble, and lift some more, and in the morning, we go to class. And in that class, we are nothing more than students. It's about pride—in ourselves, in our school. It's about our love and passion for the game. And when it's over, when we walk off that court or field for the last time, our hearts crumble. Those tears are real. But deep down inside, we are very proud of ourselves. We will forever be what few can claim...college athletes."

Sean Sornsin (baseball) / Cornell College, Iowa
First appeared in The Cornellian, December 3, 1999

159

Regardless of what division your program competes in, college softball will be one of the most fantastic and memorable experiences of your life… if you let it. But as I said at the beginning, once it's gone, it's gone forever.

You've read this book for advice on surviving your rookie season. Now, here is the most important advice of all: Don't just dabble in softball. Don't just dip your toes in the water. Dive in head-first and give yourself entirely over to the experience! Commit your entire being to the sport and to the team and soak up all that college softball has to offer.

Love being a college softball player. Love all of it! Love the games and the road trips and the hours stuck on busses and vans and the fancy team meals and the awful box lunches. Love the days when you train in the blistering sun and the pouring rain and the freezing cold of March. Love the shiny uniforms and the smelly locker rooms and the balls of newspaper you stuff inside your wet cleats. Love playing in the empty parks and the full stadiums. Love the pain of preseason and the nights packed in ice and the pride of finishing that one last repetition that you thought would kill you. Love the aching, burning, screaming in your legs on a fitness day. Love the heartbreak of a last inning loss and the joy of a win in extra innings. Love your teammates and their selflessness and courage and their habits that annoy you and their music that you can't stand. Love the fans that support you and the coaches that drive you. Don't just exist at softball; love it!

Give your very best to college softball and it will repay you a hundred times over. You've got this one last chance to be a part of a team that will forever remain truly special to you. You've got four years to be your very best softball self. Don't spend three of those years giving something less than your best and then scrambling to make amends during your senior year. You'll never regret what you gave to softball; you'll only regret what you didn't give.

As a college softball player, you'll play roughly 140 games. That's all. That's all the meaningful softball you have left. When your career finishes, make sure that you aren't left regretting a single one of those games. Make sure that you are left with a clear conscience about the effort you gave and the teammate you were each and every day.

Congratulations! Your fantastic adventure is about to begin. You may be just a rookie, but your time is now. Show the world that you are up to this challenge. This is your time to show everyone exactly what you're made of. In other words, Rookie… Get some!

A FINAL WORD

Thank you for reading my book! I hope that you feel you've gotten your money's worth.

If you would like to place a bulk order of twenty or more copies of ROOKIE at a discounted price, just email me at softballcoachfred@gmail.com.

ROOKIE is my way of giving something back to this game that has given so much to me, particularly a wealth of treasured relationships that I will forever cherish. I'm acutely aware that a player reading this book today may be tomorrow's opponent of the university I gave forty-one seasons of my life. That's all well and good. I want every player to have a college softball experience that is rewarding and memorable and filled with amazing adventures! I guess what I'm trying to say is that you've just been given a lot of really good advice. Please use it to your advantage.

If you feel you've gotten your money's worth from *ROOKIE*, I would be honored if you would take thirty seconds to leave me a five-star review. That's the best gift you can possibly give an author. It'll take almost none of your time but it will mean the world to me. Thank you in advance!

As for *ROOKIE*, I'm inviting you to participate in a little experiment. I'd love to hear about any moments during your rookie season that reminded you of this book, particularly if it helped to steer you in the right direction. Just send your story or any other feedback to:
softballcoachfred@gmail.com

I'd like to thank my many good friends, my family —June, Andrea and Mike —and my players, all who have made my coaching career a fabulous experience. Thanks to all the assistant coaches who kept me in line and offered winning advice. Thank you to my co-workers who always made time to bounce around ideas with me. I had an incredible run in college athletics and you all were a big reason why.

Thank you to my co-author, Dan Blank, for helping me cross one off the bucket list.

And just as an FYI, every awesome student-athlete who played four years of college softball for me began as a ROOKIE.

Best wishes,
Coach Fred

ABOUT THE AUTHORS

Fred Dohrmann served as Widener University's Head Soccer Men's Coach for twenty-three seasons and as the Head Softball Coach for forty-one seasons. As a college softball coach, his accomplishments include:

- 697 WINS
- NO. 22 IN NCAA D-III HISTORY IN WINS
- MOST WINS IN A SINGLE WIDENER SPORT
- SIXTEEN 20-WIN SEASONS
- 2017 MAC COMMONWEALTH TITLE
- 2017 NCAA TOURNAMENT APPEARANCE
- WILLIAM DAVID ECKARD JR AWARD WINNER

Dan Blank is the author of the #1 bestseller, *Soccer iQ,* and has been coaching college soccer for thirty years. He is the first coach in Southeastern Conference history to lead the conference's best defense in consecutive years at different universities (Ole Miss 2009, Georgia 2010). He has an 'A' License from the USSF and an Advanced National Diploma from the NSCAA. You can buy his books and read his blog at www.soccerpoet.com.

OTHER BEST-SELLING BOOKS
BY DAN BLANK

SOCCER iQ VOLUME 1 –The #1 bestseller and an NSCAA Soccer Journal Top 5 Book of the Year. The only how-to book written specifically for soccer players. Download the free companion quiz at www.soccerpoet.com.

SOCCER iQ VOLUME 2 –More simple and effective strategies for becoming a smarter soccer player.

EVERYTHING YOUR COACH NEVER TOLD YOU BECAUSE YOU'RE A GIRL –This is what your coaches would have said to you if you were a boy, told through the story of a small-college team that won more games than it ever had a right to win. It's a straightforward look at the qualities that define the most competitive females.

HAPPY FEET –*How to Be a Gold Star Soccer Parent (Everything the Coach, the Ref and Your Kid Want You to Know)* –If you want to maintain your sanity as a coach, *HAPPY FEET* is the best gift you can give a soccer parent! This book includes free companion videos to explain some of soccer's more mysterious concepts such as the advantage rule, offside, soccer systems and combination play. It also explains the most common errors that well-meaning soccer parents make without even realizing it. Prevent headaches before they start by getting soccer parents to read this book.

HIGH PRESSURE –*How to Win Soccer Games by Smothering Your Opponent* –The essential blueprint for teaching your team how to play an organized and effective style of pressing soccer.

IN MY TRIBE –*Developing a Culture of Kickass in Female Athletes* –The follow-up to *Everything Your Coach Never Told You Because You're a Girl*, this book details the specific tools we employed to feed our competitive beast.

POSSESSION –*Teaching Your Team to Keep the Darn Ball* –A book for coaches of all levels who want their teams to pass the ball and pass it well. It combines a thorough explanation of possession concepts with 30 practical possession exercises to help your team develop its ability to keep the ball. Easy-to-understand diagrams help you visualize the layout and design of these exercises. More importantly, the exercises include explanations about the critical coaching points *and* the most common mistakes the players will make when playing these exercises.

ROOKIE –*Surviving Your Freshman Year of College Soccer* –The ultimate survival guide for the rising college freshman.

Shutout Pizza –*Smarter Soccer Defending for Players and Coaches* –The book that started a #hashtag, and the essential guide for organizing your defense.

Made in the USA
Middletown, DE
29 June 2023

34190591R00106